365

SCIENCE

Projects & Activities

Phyllis J. Perry
Peter Rillero, Ph.D.

Consultant:
Joseph Peters, Ph.D.

Illustrators:
Ellen Joy Sasaki
Terri and Joe Chicko

Publications International, Ltd.

Louis Weber, C.E.O.
Publications International, Ltd.
7373 North Cicero Avenue
Lincolnwood, Illinois 60646.

Permission is never granted for commercial purposes.

Manufactured in U.S.A.

8 7 6 5 4 3 2 1

ISBN: 0-7853-1592-6

Illustrations: Ellen Joy Sasaki, Terri and Joe Chicko

Cover Photography: Brian Warling

Models: Royal Model Management: James Randle, Christine Schwass

Stylist: Cindy Zahn

Phyllis J. Perry, Ed.D., is an award-winning, full-time freelance writer with over 40 years of experience as a teacher and administrator for elementary to university graduate students. She has written several educational science books, including *Getting Started in Science Fairs* and *A Teacher's Science Companion.*

Peter Rillero, Ph.D., is an Assistant Professor in Science Education at Arizona State University West and is the consulting editor for the journal *Science Activities.* He has served as the assistant to the editor for the *Journal of Science Teacher Education,* and he has taught science as a Peace Corps Volunteer in Kenya and in the New York Public Schools.

Joseph Peters, Ph.D., is an Associate Professor, Graduate Faculty of Elementary and Middle Level Education, at The University of West Florida. He is the executive secretary of the Association for the Education of Teachers in Science and edits the *Journal of Elementary Science Education.*

CONTENTS

EVERYDAY SCIENCE

When some people think of science, they think of boring textbooks and complicated formulas. Actually, science is just a way of looking at the world around us and at the things we find in it every day.

When you mix yourself a glass of chocolate milk, you're causing a physical reaction between two chemicals. When you rub your feet on the library carpet and shock one of your classmates, you're using your body as a conductor of static electricity. When you stop to watch a line of ants carry cookie crumbs to their nest, you are observing the behavior of a species in their natural habitat.

Science is really just a system created by people to gather and organize information. We use it as one way to describe and understand the world around us.

Science has many different branches, or subjects. Chemistry deals with substances, what they are made of, what characteristics they have, and how they react with each other. Physics has to do with matter and energy; it covers things such as force, motion, heat, and light. Scientists study living things in biology, zoology, botany, and medicine; together these are called life sciences. Earth sciences, such as geology and meteorology, look at the way the Earth developed and how it changes around us. Astronomy is the study of stars, planets, and objects in space.

No matter what subject scientists study, they follow certain steps to make it more likely that their work is accurate. They usually begin their work by *observing*. They look at the world around them to see what is there and how things act. When they can, they take *measurements* as a way to describe what they see. Next, they try to *classify*, or organize, the information in a way that makes sense to them. Doing this can make it easier to understand the information. Scientists then take what they have learned and use it to form a *hypothesis* about what they are studying. A hypothesis is a guess based on facts that offers an explanation for what has been observed. To find out if a hypothesis is correct, scientists try to *test* it by doing more observation or by performing an experiment. Whether or not a hypothesis is correct, scientists can still learn by testing it.

The projects and activities in this book will help you learn how science describes the world you live in.

They will also help you learn how to study the world the way scientists do. Most of them will also be a way for you to have fun.

Before you start any of the projects in this book, you should know a couple of things. Each project has one or more test tubes by it. These show how difficult

simple   **medium**   **challenging**

the project is. Simple projects get one test tube, medium projects get two, and challenging projects get three. If you'd like to do one of the challenging projects but think it might be too hard, get help from a parent or from an older brother or sister.

Some projects also contain a Caution. These projects involve things such as flames, hazardous chemicals, or sharp objects. You should do them only with an adult's help. You should always get permission from an adult to do any project, even if it doesn't have a Caution.

Part of being a scientist is being responsible in what you do. Always use care when doing a project. Don't leave an experiment unattended unless you're sure it is safe to do so. If you have pets or younger brothers and sisters, be sure that the project poses no danger to them. Make sure you always clean up after

an experiment and dispose of material properly. This is true whether you're working in the house or outside.

After you pick a project to do, read the entire project so you know exactly what you'll have to do. Make sure that you have all the materials you will need. Most of the projects in this book use items you can find in your house. Some of them need unusual materials, such as glycerin or electrical wire. You may need to make a special trip to the store for these before you can do a project. Also, make sure that you have time to do the project you select. Some projects can be done in just a few minutes, but others have to sit for hours, days, or even weeks, and you'll need to take care of the projects during that time.

Some projects may turn out differently than you expected. That happens to all scientists. If it does happen to you, try to figure out why. Do the experiments again, or change them in some way to see if that makes a difference. Do this with projects that work the way you expected, also. Figure out why they worked, and change them in some way so that you change the results. See if you can come up with some experiments of your own, too. The best way for you, or any scientist, to learn is in a way that makes sense to you.

CHEMISTRY CONNECTIONS

In chemistry, we study matter, its properties, its structure, and the way it acts. In this chapter, you'll learn some of the ways that materials interact with each other. You'll explore the differences between physical changes and chemical reactions, and you'll also learn how to study the characteristics of different materials.

Liquid Density

Density has to do with how tightly packed an object is. If two substances have the same weight, but one takes up more space, the larger one is less tightly packed, or less *dense*. A less dense object will float on, or be supported by, a more dense object.

HEAVY WATER, HEAVIER SALTWATER

What You'll Learn: Different liquids have different densities.

What You'll Need: measuring cup; water; scale; pen and paper; large container; salt

Fill a measuring cup with 1 cup of water. Use a scale to measure how much the water weighs, and write down the weight. Pour the water into a large container, and add a little bit more water to it. Mix as much salt into the water as it will hold. Pour the saltwater into the measuring cup so that you have 1 cup of very salty water. Use the scale to measure how much the saltwater weighs. Which weighs more, the freshwater or the saltwater?

What Happened? The saltwater and freshwater you weighed each took up the same amount of space. This means that they had the same *volume*. However, one of them weighed more than the other, or was more dense. When two substances have the same volume but different weights, we say that their *density* is different; the heavier substance has a greater density. In this case, the saltwater was more dense than the freshwater. If you had difficulty proving this with this activity, try the activity Layered Look on page 10.

POP UP AND POP DOWN

Fill a basin, bathtub, aquarium, or other large container with water. Place several unopened cans of different kinds of soda into the water. Some of the cans will be heavier, or more dense, than water, and some will be less dense than water. The less dense cans will float, and the more dense cans will sink. Watch the cans, and note which ones float and which ones sink. What's the difference between the floaters and the sinkers? Do you think the cans are different or the soda is different? Can you form a hypothesis about which types of soda tend to sink and which types float? Use some other brands of soda to test your hypothesis.

If you add salt to the water, the water will become more dense. Can you predict how this might affect the cans of soda? Add salt to the water to see if your prediction was correct.

3 EGG-CITING LEVITATION

What You'll Learn: The liquids inside an egg are more dense than water so the egg sinks in water. Adding salt to the solution will make the egg rise.

What You'll Need: container; water; egg; salt; stirrer

Fill a container with enough water to cover an egg. Place the egg in the water. Does the egg float or sink? The egg sinks because it is more dense than the water. Now add salt to the water, and stir gently, being careful not to break the egg. Keep adding salt until the egg floats. You will need about 4 tablespoons of salt for every 1½ cups of water.

What Happened? Adding salt to water makes the water more dense. When enough salt is added, the egg will be less dense than the water. The egg will rise. You have produced the levitation of an egg!

 # VIVA SOUTH AMERICA! 4

What You'll Learn: Vegetable oil, corn syrup, and water have different densities.

What You'll Need: red and blue food color; corn syrup; two containers; water; measuring cup; tall, thin glass; vegetable oil

Mix ½ cup of corn syrup with red food color in a container and mix ½ cup of water with blue food color in another container. Two or three drops of food color will be enough. Pour enough red syrup into a glass to fill it about one third of the way. Next gently pour the same amount of water into the glass. Then gently pour the same amount of natural yellow vegetable oil into the glass. You'll have three distinct layers that form the color pattern used in the flags of several South American countries, such as Venezuela, Colombia, and Ecuador. Find flags from other countries, and duplicate their patterns using different food colors.

What Happened? The syrup was more dense than the other solutions so it stayed at the bottom. The oil was less dense so it floated on top of the other layers.

LAYERED LOOK

5

What You'll Learn: Freshwater floats on top of saltwater because it is less dense.
What You'll Need: water; salt; measuring cup and spoons; four clear glasses; food color; eyedropper or spoon

Make up some saltwater using about 1 cup of water and 3 or 4 tablespoons of salt in a clear glass. Pour half of your saltwater into another glass, and add food color. Take a glass of freshwater from the tap (this should be the same temperature as the saltwater). Using an eyedropper, put a small amount of colored saltwater on top of the clear freshwater. The saltwater sinks to the bottom. Get another glass of freshwater, and add some food color to it. Using the eyedropper, add a small amount of the colored freshwater to the top of the clear saltwater. The freshwater stays at the top.

What Happened? A substance with less density will float on top of a substance with more density. The freshwater floats on top of the saltwater because it is less dense. Likewise, the saltwater sinks in freshwater because it is more dense.

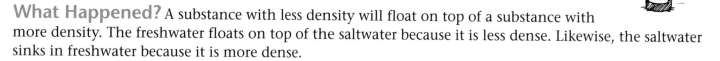

LAYERED LOOK: HOT AND COLD

6

What You'll Learn: Hot water floats on top of cold water because it is less dense.
What You'll Need: hot water; cold water; four clear cups; red and blue food color; eyedropper or spoon

Fill a cup halfway with hot water and another cup halfway with cold water. In a third cup, add red food color to some hot water. In a fourth cup, add blue food color to some cold water. Using an eyedropper, put a little red hot water into the cup of clear cold water. The red hot water stays at the top. Using the eyedropper, put a little blue cold water into the cup of clear hot water. The blue cold water sinks to the bottom.

What Happened? Hot water floats on top of cold water because it is less dense. Likewise, cold water sinks in hot water because it is more dense. Heated molecules have more energy than cool molecules. The energy of warm molecules causes them to move farther apart from each other. This makes them less dense.

DROP IT—SLOWLY!

7

In the previous project, you saw that hot water was less dense than cold water, but what about ice? The density of a substance changes depending on temperature because the volume of the substance changes with temperature. *Volume* is a measure of how much space a substance takes up, and as volume increases, density decreases. Most often, things have a greater volume when they are warmer and a lesser volume when they are colder; the same amount of a substance will take up more space when it's warm than it does when it's cold. Water is sometimes an exception to this rule, though; it actually has greater volume and less density when it's frozen than when it's liquid. You can use this fact to perform a very simple, but very cool, demonstration.

Fill a clear bowl halfway with corn oil, drop an ice cube in it, and sit back and watch. You'll notice right away that the ice cube floats on top of the oil. This is because the ice weighs less than the amount of oil needed to fill up the same volume. Eventually, the ice will melt and form drops of water. The liquid water has a lesser volume than the frozen water; the same amount takes up less space. This means that the liquid water is more dense than the frozen water; it is also more dense than the oil. The drops of water will form almost perfect spheres, and they will sink slowly to the bottom of the oil.

BOTTLED SEA: CATCH A WAVE

8

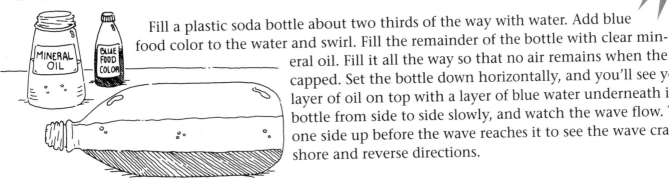

Fill a plastic soda bottle about two thirds of the way with water. Add blue food color to the water and swirl. Fill the remainder of the bottle with clear mineral oil. Fill it all the way so that no air remains when the bottle is capped. Set the bottle down horizontally, and you'll see you get a layer of oil on top with a layer of blue water underneath it. Tilt the bottle from side to side slowly, and watch the wave flow. Try tilting one side up before the wave reaches it to see the wave crash on shore and reverse directions.

Acids and Bases

In chemistry, materials can be grouped by their properties, or characteristics. One property is pH, which tells you whether a substance is an acid, a base, or a neutral. The pH values of materials are extremely important in chemistry, but also in areas such as gardening, fish keeping, cooking, and construction. We measure pH on a scale of 1 to 14, where 7 is neutral, 1 is the most acidic, and 14 is the most basic. When doing these projects, be careful handling the materials; some of them can stain or damage clothing.

9 CABBAGE PATCH CHEMIST

What You'll Learn: The color of purple cabbage changes in response to acids or bases.
What You'll Need: purple cabbage; knife; pot; water; measuring cup; stove; strainer; jar; two clear cups; vinegar; clear ammonia

Caution: *This project requires adult supervision.*

Chop some purple cabbage into small pieces. Put it into a pot with 2 cups of water, and bring it to a boil on the stove. Reduce the heat, and let it simmer for 10 minutes. The water will turn purplish. Remove the pot from the heat. Allow the purplish liquid to cool. Strain the cabbage, and pour the liquid into a jar.

Pour some of the purple liquid into two clear cups. Pour vinegar into one cup, and note the color change. Pour ammonia into the other cup, and note the color change.

What Happened? Vinegar is an acid. It caused the color of the cabbage juice to change from blue to a more reddish color. Ammonia is a weak base. It caused the color to change to green. Cabbage juice can be used to tell if chemicals are acids or bases.

10 WHAT AM I, ACID OR BASE?

What You'll Learn: Some household materials are acids and others are bases.

What You'll Need: household items, such as aspirin, milk, clear vinegar, orange juice, apple juice, soda pop, antacids, milk of magnesia, coffee, baking soda, shampoo; purple cabbage juice (see Cabbage Patch Chemist on page 12), litmus paper, or other pH indicators

Caution: *This project requires adult supervision.*

Gather up household materials such as the ones listed above. Use the purple cabbage juice or another pH indicator to test the materials to see if they are acid, base, or neutral. After you've tested a few materials, see if you can predict whether the next one will be an acid, a base, or a neutral. Think about what the substance is used for and how it smells before you make your prediction.

NEUTRALIZE ME 11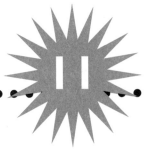

What You'll Learn: Acids and bases can produce neutral solutions when they are combined.

What You'll Need: vinegar; ammonia; three clear cups; purple cabbage juice (see Cabbage Patch Chemist on page 12), litmus paper, or other pH indicators

Put a small amount of vinegar and a small amount of ammonia in two small, clear cups. Use the purple cabbage juice or other pH indicator to test the vinegar and ammonia to see if they are acid, base, or neutral. Then mix some vinegar and ammonia together in another cup, and use your pH indicator to see if the new mixture is an acid, a base, or a neutral. Can you mix the vinegar and ammonia together in the correct amount to make a completely neutral mixture?

INVENT YOUR OWN ACID-BASE INDICATOR

12

What You'll Learn: Colors in some flowers and fruits may change in response to acids or bases.

What You'll Need: different-colored fruits, vegetables, and flower petals (lilies, asters, irises, daisies, or petunias); small jars; rubbing alcohol; several small containers; vinegar; clear ammonia

Caution: *This project requires adult supervision.*

Find some fruit, vegetables, and colored flower petals. Put them in small jars with rubbing alcohol, and leave them for 30 to 60 minutes. Pour off each of the colored solutions into two containers. With each solution, add some vinegar (an acid) to one container and some ammonia (a base) to the other. If the color of the substance changes, the substance is an acid-base indicator. Compare your results for different flowers and fruits to determine which one is the best acid-base indicator.

13

WORKING ON EGG SHELLS

Place an egg in a jar, and pour in enough vinegar to completely cover the egg. Cover the mouth of the jar securely, and leave it for 24 to 48 hours. Look at the egg.

Carefully pick it up. How has the egg changed? The vinegar reacts with the calcium in the shell and leaves the egg with no shell. Bet you never thought you could pick up an egg with no shell on it!

ACID RAIN IS A PAIN

14

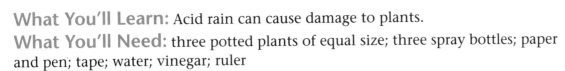

What You'll Learn: Acid rain can cause damage to plants.

What You'll Need: three potted plants of equal size; three spray bottles; paper and pen; tape; water; vinegar; ruler

Find a place where you can grow three potted plants for several weeks; make sure the plants will all experience the same growing conditions—sunlight, temperature, and so on. Label the plants and three spray bottles "REGULAR RAIN," "ACID RAIN," and "EXTREME ACID RAIN." Fill the regular rain bottle with tap water. Fill the acid rain bottle two thirds of the way with tap water and one third of the way with vinegar. Fill the extreme acid rain bottle one third of the way with tap water and two thirds of the way with vinegar. Measure and record the heights of the plants. Water each plant with the type of rain indicated on its label. Every week, measure the growth of the three plants. After a few weeks, compare the effects that the different types of rain had on the plants.

Chemical Reactions

Matter is made of *molecules*. Molecules are the smallest particles of a substance that still have the same properties as the original substance. How small is a molecule? It is way too small to be seen. Chemists study how molecules interact. Sometimes molecules interact with each other, but they remain the same. This is a physical change. Other times they interact, and the molecules change to form new molecules. This is a chemical change.

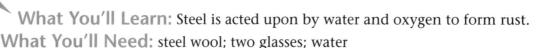

15 RUST STEALS STEEL WOOL

What You'll Learn: Steel is acted upon by water and oxygen to form rust.

What You'll Need: steel wool; two glasses; water

Take two 1-inch balls of steel wool, and put each one into a glass. Add water in one glass so it covers half of the ball. Do not add water to the other glass. Observe both pieces of steel wool after a few days. Rust has formed on the wet steel wool but not on the dry steel wool. This is oxidation, and it is an example of a chemical reaction. The iron molecules in the steel wool combine with oxygen molecules to form rust molecules (ferric oxide). This is a chemical change because it creates new molecules. The presence of water made it easier for the oxygen from the air to attach to the iron. This is why the moist steel wool rusted but the dry steel wool did not.

APPLE SCIENCE

16

What You'll Learn: The inside of an apple will undergo a chemical change when exposed to oxygen. Lemon juice will prevent this reaction from happening, but it will not reverse it.

What You'll Need: apple; knife; cotton swabs; lemon juice; water; paper towel; clock

Caution: *This project requires adult supervision.*

Cut an apple in half. Cut each half into three sections, giving you six wedges of apple. Use a cotton swab to paint lemon juice on the white fleshy parts of three wedges. Paint water on the white fleshy parts of the other three. Place the apple wedges on a paper towel, and observe them every 15 minutes for a few hours. Write your observations.

What Happened? The apples that were soaked in water turned brown when exposed to air. This is a chemical reaction called oxidation, in which oxygen combines with other molecules. The apples soaked in lemon juice did not change color. The juice prevented oxidation. Put some lemon juice on apples that have become oxidized. Does the lemon juice reverse the reaction? The lemon juice prevented the reaction, but it cannot reverse it once it has occurred. It is usually not very easy to reverse a chemical reaction.

MATCH MADE IN HEAVEN

What You'll Learn: Burning matches make a product that will cause them to stick together.

Caution: *This project requires adult supervision.*

Put the heads and bodies of two wooden matches together. Strike one match against a lighting surface. Both matches will start blazing. Then blow out both matches, and observe that the two sticks have united to become one.

What Happened? The head of a match burns, or oxidizes, when oxygen combines with the material at the head of the match. The combustion produces a new substance—a cinder type of material with holes and pockets. When the matches are burned together, the cinder material of the two matches combines and holds the matches together.

IT'S A GAS, GAS, GAS

What You'll Learn: Vinegar and baking soda mixed together produce a chemical reaction and release carbon dioxide.

What You'll Need: balloon; baking soda; measuring spoon; small bottle; vinegar

Blow up a balloon a few times to stretch the rubber. Put 3 tablespoons of baking soda into a small bottle. Pour enough vinegar into the bottle to cover the baking soda. Stretch the open end of the balloon over the mouth of the bottle. The baking soda and vinegar produce carbon dioxide gas when they combine, and the gas will rise and fill the balloon partway.

19

FOAM HOME

What You'll Learn: Vinegar and baking soda produce a chemical reaction and release carbon dioxide. The carbon dioxide gas can produce a physical change in soap.

What You'll Need: baking soda; measuring cup and spoon; bowl; dish-washing liquid; vinegar

Place about 4 tablespoons of baking soda in a bowl. Put one squirt of dish-washing liquid on the baking soda. Pour in ¼ cup of vinegar. The baking soda and vinegar chemically react to produce carbon dioxide gas. This gas causes the dish-washing liquid to produce millions of bubbles. This physical change produces foam.

ENOUGH TO MAKE YOUR MILK CURDLE

20

What You'll Learn: Acid makes milk curdle. This process is a chemical reaction.

What You'll Need: vinegar or lemon juice; skim milk; measuring cup and spoon

Place 2 teaspoons of vinegar or lemon juice into ½ cup of skim milk. Stir the milk, and observe the clumps that form. You have just witnessed milk curdling. The proteins in the milk have reacted with the acid and undergone a chemical change.

BROWN AND BLUE

21

What You'll Learn: Iodine reacts with starch to make a blue solution.

What You'll Need: iodine; water; measuring cup; eyedropper or spoon; cornstarch; assorted foods such as bread, potatoes, and cooked rice

Caution: *Iodine is a poison. Keep it away from your mouth, and wash your hands after using it.*

Make an iodine solution by adding about 10 drops of tincture of iodine to ½ cup of water. Using an eyedropper, place a drop of the iodine solution on a pile of cornstarch. Note the change in color. The fact that iodine turns blue in the presence of starch makes it a good way to see if foods contain starch. Place the iodine on bread and other foods to see if they contain starch. The iodine is called an indicator solution, because it indicates the presence of starch.

Energy and Chemical Reactions

Some chemical reactions will take place whenever the materials involved come in contact with each other. Other reactions need additional sources of energy to start the reaction. This energy can come from many sources and be supplied in many forms, including light and heat. In this section, you will use energy from lightbulbs, stoves, warm water, toasters, and eggbeaters to energize chemical reactions.

22 CARAMEL CHEMISTRY

What You'll Learn: Heat can cause a chemical change to sugar.

What You'll Need: sugar; measuring cup; nonstick pan; stove; large spoon; water

Caution: *This project requires adult supervision.*

Place about ½ cup of sugar into a deep nonstick pan. Place the pan on the stove over low heat. Continuously stir the sugar as you gradually increase the heat. Eventually, the sugar will melt and break down to form carbon. Caramel is a combination of sugar and carbon. Remove the pan from the heat when the sugar is straw colored. The sugar has been converted to caramel through a chemical reaction. If you heat the sugar too long, all the sugar turns the dark brown color of carbon and loses all of its sweetness—an interesting chemical change, but not very tasty!

Now you will dissolve the caramel in water to make it taste better. This is a physical change.

Slowly add ½ cup of water to the caramel. Don't add this too quickly, as the caramel is hot and might splatter the water and burn you. Place the pan back on the stove over low heat, and stir the mixture until the caramel dissolves in the water. When it has cooled, taste the mixture. The caramel tastes different from the original white sugar because it is a different substance.

TOP SECRET INVISIBLE INK

23

What You'll Learn: Heat can cause a chemical change.

What You'll Need: toothpick; lemon juice; paper; heat source, such as a lightbulb or iron

Caution: *This project requires adult supervision.*

Dip the round side of a toothpick into lemon juice, and write a secret message with it on a piece of paper. Use lots of lemon juice for each letter you write. Allow the paper to dry until you can't see the writing any more. Now move the paper back and forth over a heat source. As the ink gets warm, your message is revealed.

What Happened? The acid in the lemon juice breaks down the cellulose of the paper into sugars. The heat supplied tends to caramelize the sugars, making them brown and revealing the secret writing. Repeat this activity with vinegar or milk to find out which makes the best invisible ink.

 # WHIP IT GOOD

24

What You'll Learn: Beating egg whites causes the protein in them to denature.

What You'll Need: egg; bowl; whisk or electric beater

Separate the yolk from the white of an egg, and put the egg whites in a bowl. The whites consist of long protein molecules wound up like balls of yarn. Beat the egg whites with a whisk or electric beater. In time, you will produce a meringue (MER-ANG). The energy you supplied with the whisk unraveled the balls of protein and changed the properties of the egg white. Changing proteins this way is called *denaturing*.

YOU'RE TOAST!

25

What You'll Learn: The production of charcoal is a chemical reaction that is dependent upon heat.

What You'll Need: bread; toaster

Place bread into a toaster, and toast it a little longer than usual. Observe the charcoal that is produced on the bread. In this chemical reaction, the carbohydrates of the bread combine with oxygen. Heat is necessary to produce the oxidation of the bread.

CHILL OUT

26

What You'll Learn: Heat is a necessary part of the chemical reaction that occurs when a candle burns.

What You'll Need: aluminum foil; scissors; candle; matches; tongs

Caution: *This project requires adult supervision.*

Cut a square of aluminum foil about 4 inches by 4 inches. In the middle of one side, cut a thin slit going to the middle of the square. Light a candle. Notice the burning of the flame. You are watching a chemical reaction. The heat causes the wax to be converted into simpler products, and this produces more heat, which causes the reaction to continue. Now cool things off a bit. Using tongs to hold the aluminum foil, carefully position the foil so the candle flame is inside the slit. Watch as the candle goes out.

What Happened? The aluminum foil absorbs and reflects the heat of the flame. This pulls heat from the flame and from the candle. The heat needed to continue the chemical reaction was taken away, so the reaction stopped.

EAT, YEAST, AND BE MERRY

27

What You'll Learn: Yeast break down sugar for energy. They do this in a chemical reaction that is aided by heat.

What You'll Need: two glasses; dry yeast; measuring cup and spoon; sugar; water

In each of two glasses, place ¼ teaspoon of dry yeast and 4 teaspoons of sugar. Add ¾ cup of cold water to one glass and ¾ cup of warm (not above 130°F) water to the other glass. Compare what happens to the yeast in the two glasses.

What Happened? With the aid of heat, the yeast in the warm cup was able to break down the sugar, giving off alcohol and carbon dioxide. The carbon dioxide bubbled up in the solution. Without the added heat, the yeast in the cold glass could not break down the sugar. When people bake bread, they add yeast to flour and put it in a warm place. The yeast breaks down sugar and releases carbon dioxide, and the gas causes the bread to rise.

Physical Changes

Just as in a chemical change, a physical change occurs when two substances
interact or when energy is applied to one or more substances. Unlike a chemical change,
though, the molecules of a substance stay the same after a physical change;
no new substance is formed. Physical changes can make a substance look
different in size, shape, or color.

28 SALT SOLUTION

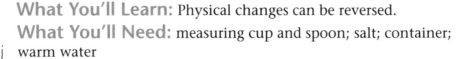

What You'll Learn: Physical changes can be reversed.

What You'll Need: measuring cup and spoon; salt; container; warm water

Put 2 teaspoons of salt in a container. Add about ¼ cup of warm water, and observe as the salt dissolves in the water and becomes invisible. This is a physical change. Place the container in a warm spot where evaporation will occur quickly. Allow the solution to stand for three days so the water will evaporate. Notice that the salt is left behind. This is also a physical change. The physical change of dissolving the salt in water was reversed by the second physical change of the water evaporating.

LEONARDO DA SALTY  29

What You'll Learn: Salt and food color will both dissolve in water (a physical change). If the water evaporates, it leaves the salt and the food color behind (also a physical change).

What You'll Need: warm water; salt; several containers; several different food colors; paper; paint brushes or cotton swabs

Mix warm water and salt together in several containers; add as much salt to each solution as it will hold. Add a different food color to each container, and mix well. Paint a picture on paper using the colored salt solutions. Put it on thick so that when it dries, a lot of salt will be left behind. Let the painted paper sit for several hours until the water evaporates, and then observe. Notice how the color and salt remain on the paper. The interesting patterns of color around the salt crystals create a beautiful picture.

30 DRIED FRUIT: APPLE CHIPS

What You'll Learn: Removing water (dehydration) from fruit is a physical change.

What You'll Need: two apples (or similar fruit); scale; pen and paper; knife; plate

Caution: *This project requires adult supervision.*

Weigh two apples on a scale, and record their weight. Slice the apples into thin slices. Spread them on a plate, and leave them out for three days.

On the third day, observe the apple slices. How have they changed? Weigh all the slices. How does the weight of the dried slices compare with the original weight of the apples? They weigh less because the apples have lost water through evaporation. This is an example of a physical change.

SHRUNKEN HEADS 31

What You'll Learn: Removing water (dehydration) from a peeled apple is a physical change that causes a change in the size and shape of the apple.

What You'll Need: apple; potato peeler; knife; string

Caution: *This project requires adult supervision.*

In the previous activity, you learned that the inside of an apple can lose water due to evaporation. Now you are going to have some more fun with this idea. Peel the skin from an apple with a potato peeler. Using a knife, carve a face into the apple. Hang the apple with a string tied to the stem, and let it dry for three days. Observe the shriveled-up appearance of the apple. It has lost water through evaporation. This is a physical change. Observe the face you carved into the apple. It looks shriveled-up like a shrunken head or a witch's face that you could use as a Halloween decoration.

32 GUNK

What You'll Learn: Cornstarch mixed with water has properties of both a liquid and a solid.

What You'll Need: water; measuring cup; bowl; cornstarch; spoon

Pour 1 cup of water into a bowl. Add cornstarch a little at a time, stirring as you go. You will need about 1½ cups of cornstarch. Keep adding until it gets difficult to stir. When it is perfect, you can hit the solution with your hand and it will not splatter. Have fun with the gunk. Scoop some up, and let it dribble back into the bowl. Try to form some into a ball. Have a friend take a look. Slap your hand into the bowl, and watch as your friend jumps back expecting a splash, but no splash happens. When you've had enough fun with the gunk, throw it in the trash, but don't pour it down the drain, as it may clog the pipes.

SNOWFLAKE SCIENCE 33

What You'll Learn: It is almost impossible to find two snowflakes exactly alike. Chemically they are identical, but they have physical differences.

What You'll Need: fresh snowflakes; black paper; magnifying glass

Next time it is snowing, catch some snowflakes on a piece of black paper. Look at them carefully with a magnifying glass. Observe that all the snowflakes look different. They have different shapes and sizes, yet each is made of water. To be sure, allow the snow to melt and observe it as liquid water.

MILK IT

34

What You'll Learn: Water and oil can be mixed together to form an emulsion.

What You'll Need: two glass jars with lids; vegetable oil; water; dish-washing liquid

Fill a glass jar about one quarter of the way with vegetable oil. Pour in water until the jar is three quarters of the way full. Repeat with a second jar. Put lids on the jars securely, and shake them. The oil and water mix, but in time, the two liquids separate again, leaving the oil on top and water on the bottom. The oil floats because it is less dense than the water. Now add a squirt of dish-washing liquid to one of the jars. Shake both jars again.

What Happened? The detergent emulsifies the oil droplets, or breaks them into much smaller droplets. These small droplets remain suspended in the water and give the water a milky appearance. This kind of mixture is called an *emulsion*.

BUTTER ME UP

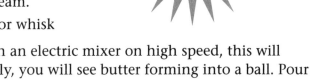

35

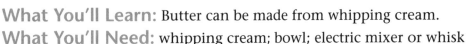

What You'll Learn: Butter can be made from whipping cream.

What You'll Need: whipping cream; bowl; electric mixer or whisk

Put a pint of whipping cream into a bowl, and whip it. With an electric mixer on high speed, this will take 7 to 9 minutes; with a whisk, it will take longer. Eventually, you will see butter forming into a ball. Pour off the liquid, and taste the butter.

What Happened? Milk contains fat, and whipping cream contains even more fat. This fat is broken into small droplets and dissolved in the water of milk to form an emulsion. The energy you added to the cream by beating it made the small droplets of fat crash into each other and form bigger drops. The larger drops crashed into each other and formed even larger drops, and so on, until you had made one big drop of fat—butter. The process where small drops combine to form big drops is called *coalescing*.

36 BALLOON B-R-R-R-R AND BALLOON SWEAT

What You'll Learn: The size of a filled balloon depends upon its temperature.

What You'll Need: pot; water; stove; bowl; ice; balloon; marker; string; ruler; paper and pen; clock or watch; tongs

Caution: *This project requires adult supervision.*

Fill a pot about halfway with water, and heat it over a medium heat on the stove. Fill a bowl about halfway with a mixture of ice and water. Blow up and knot a balloon. To measure the balloon's circumference, or the distance around it, start by marking an X at the widest part of the balloon. Wrap a string around the balloon so that it begins and ends at the X, and then measure the length of the string with a ruler. Write down this length. This is the balloon's circumference at room temperature. Put the balloon into the ice water for 3 minutes. Remove the balloon, and measure and record its circumference. Using tongs, hold the balloon in the warm water for 3 minutes; make sure the water is not too hot or the balloon will pop. Remove the balloon, and measure and record its circumference. Compare the three measurements you took of the balloon. How does temperature affect the size of the balloon?

What Happened? The balloon was smallest in cold conditions and largest in warm conditions. When an object is cold, the molecules move with less energy and pack closer together. When the molecules are warmer, they move faster and move farther apart. Thus, temperature can cause a change in the size of an object.

Curious Combinations

When materials combine, the resulting material may have different characteristics because of the way the molecules interact. In this section, you will mix different materials and observe the physical changes when these molecules meet.

OCEAN CONDUCTOR

37

What You'll Learn: Salt doesn't conduct electricity well and neither does distilled water. When mixed together, they do conduct electricity.

What You'll Need: conductivity tester (see Probing for Conductors on page 134); salt; distilled water (or water that does not have a lot of dissolved materials in it); cup; tablespoon

Using the conductivity tester, touch the probes to a pile of salt. Notice that the bulb does not light. Put the probes in a cup of distilled water, and also notice that the bulb does not light. Now combine a few tablespoons of salt into a cup of water. Put the probes into the saltwater; the bulb lights. Unlike the salt and the water separately, the saltwater solution is an electrical conductor because it has ions (charged particles) that conduct electricity.

38 BEADS ON THE BEACH

What You'll Learn: When big particles mix with smaller particles, they may take up less space than when they were separate.

What You'll Need: marbles or large beads; 2-cup measuring cup; large container; sand or dirt

Carefully measure 1 cup of marbles, and pour them into a container. Carefully measure 1 cup of sand, and combine it with the marbles in the container. Mix them around with your hand. You probably expect that you have 2 cups of the marble-sand mixture. If you pour the mixture into the measuring cup, you will see that that's not correct. Do you know why?

What Happened? The marbles have empty space around them, and the smaller sand particles can fill up that space. This makes the volume of the combined marble-sand mixture less than the combined volumes of the separate marbles and sand. This is a model for how some molecules combine when mixed.

 # SO SWEET! 39

What You'll Learn: When sugar and water are mixed, they may take up less space than when they were separate.

What You'll Need: sugar; 2-cup measuring cup; container; water; spoon

Carefully measure 1 cup of sugar, and pour it into a container. Carefully measure 1 cup of water, and add it to the sugar in the container. Mix them around with a spoon; you won't be able to dissolve all the sugar since there is not enough water. You probably expect that you have 2 cups of the sugar-water mixture. If you pour the mixture into the measuring cup, you will see that that's not correct. Do you know why?

What Happened? Water molecules are small, and sugar molecules are large. The smaller water molecules can fill in some of the empty space around the larger sugar molecules. This makes the volume of the combined substances less than the volume of the separate substances.

LESS THAN THE SUM

40

What You'll Learn: When alcohol and water are mixed, they may take up less space than when they were separate.

What You'll Need: graduated cylinder; rubbing alcohol (the closer to 100% alcohol, the more dramatic the result); large container; water

If you have a graduated cylinder, measure 50 milliliters of alcohol, and pour it into a container. Then measure 50 milliliters of water, and add it to the container. Pour the combined liquids back into the graduated cylinder, and like magic, you have less than 100 milliliters of solution.

Alternative Method:
For this method, be sure to measure everything *very* carefully. If you don't have a graduated cylinder, get a tall thin jar, such as an olive jar. Carefully measure ½ cup of water, and pour it into the olive jar. Put a piece of tape on the outside of the jar to mark the water level. Pour the water into a container. Pour alcohol into the olive jar exactly up to the tape mark. Then pour the alcohol into the container with the water, and mix them together. Now pour some of the water-alcohol mixture from the container back into the jar, filling it exactly to the tape line. Pour this out into another container. You might expect the remaining mixture in the first container to fill the jar up to the tape line. But when you pour it in, you find it falls short of the line. You have less than 1 cup of the mixture, even though you started with ½ cup of water and ½ cup of alcohol.

What Happened?
The water molecules are smaller than the alcohol molecules. The water fills in the spaces around the alcohol, and the combined liquids take up less space.

WHAT'S THE MATTER?

All physical objects are made up of matter. By studying different objects,
you'll learn that all matter has mass and that all matter takes up space.
You'll also learn how temperature and pressure affect matter.
You'll find that matter can be solid, liquid, or gas, and that the
three different kinds of matter are alike in some ways and different in others.

Matter

Every object you can think of—your shoes, flowers, rocks, your fingernails, a balloon, the sun, orange juice—is made up of matter. One of the smallest units of matter is the atom, and atoms join together to form molecules. All of the everyday objects around us are made up of matter that has joined to form molecules.

SALT TO SALT

What You'll Learn: Molecules of one kind of matter can be mixed with molecules of another kind of matter.

What You'll Need: salt; measuring spoon; dark paper; magnifying glass; hammer; glass of water

Sprinkle a teaspoon of salt onto a piece of dark paper. Study the grains of salt with a magnifying glass. What shape do they have? Put another piece of paper on top of the salt. Use a hammer to lightly crush the salt into smaller pieces. Now what sizes and shapes are the grains of salt? Pour the tiny grains of salt into a glass of water, and stir. Can you see the salt? Taste the water. Is it salty? Put the cup of water in a sunny window for a couple of days. When the water has evaporated, some salt will be left in the cup. Scrape this salt back onto the dark paper. Use your magnifying glass to study the grains again. Do they look like the grains you started with?

SHAPE SHIFTER

What You'll Learn: Liquids do not keep their own shape, but solids do.

What You'll Need: two ice cubes; plate; cup

Take two ice cubes from the freezer. Set one on a dinner plate, and set one in a cup. Notice that the ice cubes have a definite shape and that they stay in that shape. They are solids. We can't see the molecules that are in the ice, but a force is holding each molecule to the ones around it.

Watch the two ice cubes as they begin to warm up. As ice warms, the molecules begin to move faster. They slide over and around each other. When the molecules are moving fast enough, the force can't hold them in the cube shape. The ice melts and changes from a solid to a liquid.

Look at the melting ice on the plate. The liquid doesn't have a definite shape. It's a puddle on the plate. The ice in the cup melts, and the liquid flows into the same shape as the cup.

MOVING MOLECULES

43

What You'll Learn: The molecules in an object are constantly in motion.

What You'll Need: two glasses; water; food color

Fill a glass with water, and let it sit for a few minutes so the water appears still. Add a couple of drops of food color. Watch as the drops settle to the bottom of the water. Let the glass sit undisturbed for several hours. When you come back, you'll find that the food color has been spread throughout the whole glass of water. Try the project again. This time, use one glass of cold water and one glass of hot water. Check on the glasses every few minutes. Compare how long it takes the food color to spread throughout the hot water and the cold water.

What Happened? Water molecules are constantly in motion, even if it looks like the water is still. The first time you did the experiment, the moving water molecules collided with the food color molecules and started them moving. After a time, the food color molecules were spread through the glass of water. The second time you did the experiment, you found that the food color spread through the hot water faster than through the cold water. This is because the molecules in hot water move faster than the molecules in cold water. This is true for every substance.

SWEET RACERS

44

What You'll Learn: Solids can be dissolved into liquids.

What You'll Need: water; two glasses; sugar cubes; napkin; hammer

Fill two glasses halfway with warm water. Wrap a cube of sugar in a napkin. Use a hammer to gently break the sugar cube into tiny pieces of sugar. Drop a whole sugar cube into one glass of water and the crushed sugar cube into the second glass of water at the same time. In which glass does the sugar dissolve faster?

What Happened? Sugar dissolves in water when the sugar molecules are surrounded by water molecules. In the glass with the crushed sugar cube, the water molecules were able to surround the sugar molecules faster because the sugar molecules were spread out. The crushed sugar cube dissolved faster.

Density and Volume

The *density* of an object is a measurement of its heaviness. Density includes an object's mass, or weight, and its volume, or the amount of space it takes up. If two objects weigh the same, but one takes up less space, the smaller one has a greater density. Understanding density will help explain other things, such as why some objects float while other objects sink.

MAKING A DENSITY COLUMN

45

What You'll Learn: An object or substance with less density will float on top of an object or substance with greater density.

What You'll Need: cup; water; red food color; spoon; jar; turkey baster; corn syrup; glycerin; dishwashing liquid; vegetable oil; rubbing alcohol; various small objects

Fill a cup with water, add some red food color, and stir. Set a tall, narrow jar on a table. Using a turkey baster, slowly add the following to the jar in this order: corn syrup, glycerin, dish-washing liquid, colored water, vegetable oil, and rubbing alcohol. Add enough of each to fill about one sixth of the jar.

When you add each substance, put the tip of the baster on the side of the jar, and squeeze the bulb gently so the liquid slides down the side of the jar. Don't squirt it in. The liquids you've added will stay separate from each other; the less dense liquids will float on top of the more dense liquids. Take a cork, a marble, a paper clip, and several other small objects, and add them one at a time to the jar. The objects will float at different levels. Can you guess why?

46 MAKING A HYDROMETER

What You'll Learn: A hydrometer measures the density of liquids.

What You'll Need: two glasses; water; salt; measuring cup; spoon; plastic drinking straw; scissors; plasticine clay; string

Fill two glasses with water. Add ⅓ cup of salt to one of the glasses of water, and stir it with a spoon. Set both glasses on a counter while you make your hydrometer.

Cut a plastic drinking straw so that it's a little longer than your glass. Put a small ball of plasticine clay about the size of a marble at the end of the straw. Be sure that the clay makes a tight fit on the straw so that water won't leak into the straw.

Put the clay end of the straw into the glass of plain water; it should float just off the bottom. If it doesn't float, remove a little of the clay. When your straw and clay float, take the straw out of the water, and tie a piece of string around the middle of the straw. Put the straw back in the water. Slide the string to mark the water level on the straw. The straw is now a hydrometer. The higher the straw floats in a glass of liquid, the denser the liquid is.

Put your hydrometer into the glass of saltwater. Where is the string? Is saltwater more dense or less dense than freshwater? Use your hydrometer to check the density of other liquids, such as cooking oil or milk.

MARBLES IN WATER 47

What You'll Learn: An object's volume determines how much space it takes up.

What You'll Need: water; 2-cup measuring cup; 16 marbles of the same size; paper and pen

Pour 1 cup of water into a 2-cup measuring cup. Drop four marbles into the water. What is the water level in the measuring cup now? Write this down. Drop four more marbles into the water. What is the level of the water in the measuring cup now? Could you predict, using the information that you have written down, what the level of water will be when you add eight more marbles? Write down your prediction. Add eight more marbles to the cup of water. Was your prediction correct?

ROCK SPACE

48

What You'll Learn: You can measure the volume of objects with flat sides and the volume of objects that do not have flat sides.

What You'll Need: shoe box; metric ruler; paper and pen; measuring cup that indicates milliliters; small rock

Carefully measure the length, width, and height of a shoe box in centimeters. Write the measurements down, and then multiply the numbers (l×w×h). The amount you come up with will be the volume of the box in cubic centimeters.

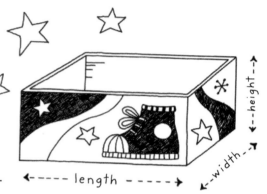

VOLUME = Length x Width x Height

How can you find the volume of something that doesn't have flat, regular sides? Fill a measuring cup with 50 milliliters of water. Gently drop a rock into the water. Now how high is the water level in the measuring cup? Subtract 50 milliliters from the new measurement. The number you come up with will be the volume of the rock in milliliters. Try with a rock of a different size. Could you use this method to find the volume of a sponge?

What Happened? When you put the rock into the water, it takes up space. That space used to have water in it, and the water has to go somewhere. The water level rises in the measuring cup by exactly the amount of space that the rock occupies.

DENSITY VS. VOLUME

49

What You'll Learn: Liquids of the same volume may not have the same density.

What You'll Need: two identical jars with lids; honey; vegetable oil; balance scale

Take two identical jars. Fill one with honey and the other with vegetable oil; put the lids on both jars. The honey and the vegetable oil have the same volume; they take up the same amount of space in the jars. Now compare their mass, or weight. Put the jar with honey on one side of a balance scale and the jar with vegetable oil on the other side. You will see that they do not balance; one of them weighs more than the other. Substances with the same volume but different weights have different densities.

States of Matter

Matter comes in three states: solid, liquid, and gas. Solids can melt into liquids. When a solid is stirred into a liquid, it sometimes disappears. When it does, we say that the solid has dissolved to form a solution. Gases can dissolve in liquids and so can other liquids. In the same way, liquids can evaporate into gases, and gases can mix into other gases.

LESS AND LESS AND LESS 50

What You'll Learn: Water evaporates into the air.

What You'll Need: measuring cup; water; two jars (one with a lid); marker

Pour 1 cup of water into a clean jar. Immediately screw the lid onto the jar. Pour 1 cup of water into a second jar, but do not put a lid on this jar. Place both jars next to each other in a sunny window. With a marker, mark the level of the water in both jars on the outside. At the end of each day, mark the level of the water. After one week, what is the difference you see between the water level in the two jars?

What Happened? Heat from the sun made the water in both jars evaporate. In the jar with the lid, the water could not escape, and it condensed back into liquid water. In the jar with no lid, the water escaped into the air when it evaporated, so there was less and less water in the jar as the week went on.

DISAPPEARING ACT

51

What You'll Learn: Solids can be dissolved in water, but different solids will dissolve in different amounts.

What You'll Need: water; measuring cup; three small jars with lids; measuring spoon; salt; sugar; flour; pen and paper

Pour ½ cup of water into each of three small jars. Add ¼ teaspoon of salt to one jar, ¼ teaspoon of sugar to the second jar, and ¼ teaspoon of flour to the third jar. Put lids on the jars, and label each jar "SALT," "SUGAR," and "FLOUR." Shake each jar well. Which of the solids dissolved in water? Continue to add ¼ teaspoons of each solid to each labeled jar until the solutions are saturated, or until no more solids will dissolve. Keep track of how much of each solid you added.

YUM! YUM! YUM!

52

What You'll Learn: When liquids evaporate into gases, they can leave material behind.

What You'll Need: pan; water; stove; sugar; measuring spoon; string; pencil; glass; scissors; button

Caution: *This project requires adult supervision.*

Bring a small pan of water to a boil on the stove. Turn off the heat. Add 1 tablespoon of sugar, and stir until it dissolves. Continue adding sugar, 1 tablespoon at a time, letting each tablespoonful dissolve completely before adding the next. When no more sugar will dissolve in the water, allow the saturated solution to cool.

Tie a string to the middle of a pencil, and set the pencil across the rim of a glass. Cut the string so that it just touches the bottom of the glass. Tie a button onto the bottom of the string. Pour the cooled sugar water into the glass. Rest the pencil across the rim of the glass so that the string and button are in the solution. Allow it to sit in a warm place without being disturbed for several days so that the water evaporates. As the water evaporates, it will leave sugar crystals on the string. You can eat these crystals like rock candy.

53 POP IN A BALLOON

What You'll Learn: Gases can dissolve in a liquid.

What You'll Need: bottle of pop; balloon; watch

Open up a bottle of soda pop, and set it on a table. Immediately slip the end of a balloon over the neck of the bottle. Pull the balloon's end well down over the bottle so that it fits tightly. Check on the balloon about every 10 minutes for any changes.

What Happened? Soda pop is carbonated. This means that carbon dioxide gas has been dissolved in the liquid under high pressure. Opening the bottle releases the pressure, and the carbon dioxide gas begins to escape from the liquid. The balloon trapped the carbon dioxide gas as it left the bottle, and then the gas inflated the balloon.

SMELLY SCIENCE 54

What You'll Learn: Perfume molecules will move through the air.

What You'll Need: two bottles of perfume; shoe box

Ask a friend to sit across the room from you. Set a bottle of perfume on a table or counter, and open it. Put a second bottle of perfume inside a shoe box. Open this perfume bottle, and quickly put the lid on the shoe box. Set the shoe box next to the first perfume bottle. Ask your friend to tell you when he or she can smell the perfume from across the room. It will take a little time for the molecules of perfume to move through the air. When your friend smells perfume, take the bottle of perfume out of the shoe box, and quickly close the shoe box again. Put the tops on both perfume bottles. Ask your friend to lift the shoe box lid and smell inside the box. The scent will be strong because the perfume molecules could not escape into the room.

Friction

Using energy creates heat. One way that energy can produce heat is through friction. When two objects rub against each other, some energy is converted to heat through friction. Applying heat to matter can cause a change in the matter.

PUMP IT UP

55

What You'll Learn: When we use energy, some of it can become heat.

What You'll Need: bicycle; bicycle pump; air pressure gauge

Take a bicycle and a bicycle pump that have been stored in a garage where it is cool. Feel the tires of the bicycle with your hands. The tires should feel cool to the touch. Feel the bicycle pump. It also feels cool to the touch. Measure the pressure in the back tire. Then let about half of the air out of the back tire. Feel both of the tires again. They should both still feel cool to your touch.

Now pump up the back tire. When it is hard and full of air, feel both of the tires again. The back tire will feel much warmer than the front tire. Feel the bicycle pump. It will feel warm, too.

What Happened? You used energy to make air move from outside the tire to inside the tire. As the air moved, its molecules bumped into the sides of the pump and the sides of the tire, causing friction. Some of your energy was used to overcome this friction. As the molecules moved against each other, they generated heat, which made the pump and the tire feel warm.

HOT TOUCH

What You'll Learn: Friction creates heat.

What You'll Need: hand towel; two plastic pens

On a camping trip or in a film, you may have seen someone start a fire by rubbing two sticks together rapidly near some tinder. The friction of the two sticks causes enough heat to spark a fire. You can do a similar experiment without starting a fire.

Take two plastic pens, and feel them. If they have been on a table or desk in your house, they will probably feel cool to the touch. Put one of the pens on a table. Take the other pen, and vigorously rub it with a hand towel for about a minute. Stop rubbing. Now hold a pen in each hand—one from the table and one that you have been rubbing. Is one of the pens hot? The friction caused by rubbing one pen in a towel generated heat and caused the rubbed pen to feel hot to the touch.

 # HOT BUTTERED POPCORN

What You'll Learn: Heat causes popcorn kernels to explode and also melts a solid piece of butter into liquid.

What You'll Need: air popper; popcorn; bowl; butter; saucepan; stove

Caution: *This project requires adult supervision.*

There is a small amount of water inside a popcorn kernel. When enough heat is applied, the water turns to steam and expands, making the kernel burst. Put some popcorn into an air popper, and turn on the popper. Position a bowl to catch the popcorn. At the same time, put half of a stick of butter in a saucepan over low heat. Soon the kernels of popcorn will pop out of the popper. The solid stick of butter will melt into a liquid. Pour the butter over the popcorn and enjoy it!

58 CURLY FISH

What You'll Learn: Warm surfaces expand more quickly than cool surfaces.

What You'll Need: celluloid; scissors; bowl of water

Cut a simple fish shape from a sheet of celluloid. Your fish should be about 4 inches long and 1 inch wide at the widest part of its body and 1 inch wide from tip to tip of its V-shaped tail. Drop the fish into a bowl of water.

Tell a friend that your fish is so lifelike that if someone picks it up out of the water, it will curl up. When your friend picks up the fish from the water and puts it in his or her hand, probably nothing will happen. But if you rub your two hands together vigorously and then ask your friend to put the fish flat on your open hand, the fish will curl its head and tail together within a few seconds.

What Happened? The friction from rubbing your hands together created heat, and the heat was passed on to the fish. However, the plastic fish did not warm evenly. The bottom part touching your warm hand warmed faster and caused the plastic to expand, but the top, colder surface remained the same. This difference in the temperature of the top and bottom sides of the fish caused it to curl.

Evaporation and Condensation

During a rainstorm, water falls from the sky. It soaks into the ground and collects in puddles. After the rain stops and the sun begins to shine again, puddles dry up and the water disappears. The sun's heat makes the water turn into a gas, which rises up in the air. This process of a liquid turning into a gas is called *evaporation*. When the temperature of water vapor is lowered enough, it becomes liquid water. This process is called *condensation*.

59 SOLAR STILL

What You'll Learn: Warmth from the sun causes moisture to evaporate from the soil.

What You'll Need: shovel; bowl; heavy clear plastic; rocks

Find a spot in your yard that gets sun in the morning, and then get permission to dig a small hole there. Use a shovel to dig a hole 1 foot deep and 18 inches wide. Place a small bowl in the bottom of the hole. Cover the hole with a piece of heavy clear plastic. Drop a small rock into the middle of the plastic cover so that it sags down and is about 2 inches above the bowl. Fasten the plastic in place all around the hole using rocks for weights. Check the hole in the late afternoon. What did you find in your bowl?

What Happened? Heat from the sun caused moisture in the soil to evaporate, or turn into a gas. The gas was trapped by the plastic cover. As the gas cooled, it turned back to liquid water and dripped into the bowl.

THE DEW POINT 60

What You'll Learn: When the temperature of water vapor drops enough, it becomes liquid water.

What You'll Need: metal can with no label; water; food color; ice cubes; spoon

Fill a clean metal can about two thirds of the way with warm water, and add a few drops of food color. Let the can sit on a table for one hour until it reaches room temperature. Add ice cubes to the water one at a time, and stir with a spoon. Watch the outside of the can. After you add enough ice cubes, the outside of the can will become wet with small droplets of clear water. Notice that the drops on the outside are clear and that the water inside the can is colored; the drops did not come from the water inside the can.

What Happened? The air outside the can contains water vapor. When the vapor in the air came in contact with the cold can, the vapor's temperature lowered, and it condensed into liquid water on the outside of the can.

DISAPPEARING PAINTINGS

61

What You'll Learn: Liquid evaporates if its temperature rises.

What You'll Need: large container; water; paintbrush

On a hot afternoon when the sun has been shining for several hours and the sidewalk is warm, take a large container of water and a clean paintbrush outside. Dip your brush into the water, and "paint" a picture on the sidewalk. You might paint a cat, a tree, a rocket ship, or anything else you like to draw. Do not be too detailed in this drawing; just make the outline, and add only a few details. Then stand back, and look at your picture. Admire it quickly because your "painting" will soon disappear. The water will evaporate into the warm air.

QUICK DRY

62

What You'll Learn: Water evaporates fastest in warm, dry places.

What You'll Need: scissors; cloth; bowl of water; pen and paper

Cut a large rag into six strips of cloth that are about the same width and length. Soak all of the strips of cloth in a bowl of water until they are completely wet.

Find six different places to put your strips of cloth, such as on a sunny window ledge, on a shelf in the refrigerator, on a tree branch in the shade, on a tree branch in the sun, in a garage wadded up on the floor, or flat on a cement surface in a sunny spot. Write the places down on a piece of paper. Think about each place, and predict where the cloth will dry the fastest. Number each place 1 through 6 on the paper, with 1 being where the cloth will dry fastest and 6 being where the cloth will dry slowest. Check the strips of cloth often. How did you do on your predictions? Why did the cloth dry fast in some places and slow in others?

63

SOLID TO LIQUID TO SOLID

What You'll Learn: Solids can change into liquids, and liquids can change into solids.

What You'll Need: can of frozen orange juice; pitcher; large spoon; water; two paper cups; two wooden craft sticks

Open a can of frozen orange juice, and spoon it into a large pitcher. Touch the frozen juice to feel that it is both solid and cold. Add water according to the package directions to make orange juice. Fill two paper cups about two thirds of the way with orange juice. Put a craft stick into the liquid in each paper cup. Being careful not to spill, put the two cups of juice into the freezer. Check them after two hours. Can you gently pull out the craft stick, or has the liquid orange juice frozen solid around the stick? If it has frozen, peel off the paper cups. You and a friend can enjoy a frozen treat!

 # WATER, WATER EVERYWHERE **64**

What You'll Learn: Cold air cannot hold as much water vapor as warm air.

By using your powers of observation, you'll be able to see several examples of condensation. Put a hand mirror in the freezer until the mirror is cold. Take the mirror out, and hold it close to your face. Blow your warm breath onto the mirror. You will see a misty spot on the mirror made from drops of water. The next time you get out of your bath or shower, look at the mirror in your bathroom. The bathroom mirror may be covered with drops of water. In both cases, where did the drops of water come from? What did temperature have to do with forming them?

Air Pressure

We live in a sea of air that we call the *atmosphere*. The atmosphere contains gases, including nitrogen and oxygen. Like all other types of matter, this air has mass and volume, and its weight can exert pressure. Its volume also changes depending on its temperature.

CAVED-IN CAN

65

What You'll Learn: Air pressure is strong enough to bend a can.

What You'll Need: large container; water; ice cubes; empty pop can; measuring cup; stove; tongs or pot holders

Caution: *This project requires adult supervision.*

Fill a large container with water and ice cubes. Set it aside to use later. Pour ½ cup of water into an empty pop can. With adult supervision, put the can on a burner on the stove. When the water in the can starts to boil, you will see steam coming from the hole in the top of the can. Turn off the stove, and use tongs or pot holders to remove the can from the heat. Quickly put the can in the container of ice water, turning it upside down to rest on its top. Watch as the can cools.

What Happened? When you heated the water in the can, it produced steam that forced the air out of the can. When you put the can in the ice water, its temperature lowered, and the steam condensed back into water. The pressure of the air outside the can was greater than the air pressure inside the can. The weight of the outside air crushed the can.

66 BURN OUT

What You'll Learn: A candle needs oxygen to burn.
What You'll Need: candle; matches; saucer; tall glass

Caution: *This project requires adult supervision.*

Take a candle that is about 4 inches long, and carefully light it with a match. Tilt the candle over a saucer so that some wax drips into the saucer. Be careful! This wax is hot! After you have a small puddle of wax in the saucer, blow out the candle. Then place the bottom of the candle into the puddle of melted wax. This wax puddle will dry and hold your candle.

Carefully light the candle again. Observe it. The candle should burn brightly. Now put a tall glass over the candle. The lip of the glass should rest on the saucer. Watch what happens. The flame will burn for a while, and then it will go out. The candle has used up all the oxygen in the glass. Without oxygen, the candle cannot burn.

FLAME OUT 67

What You'll Learn: Carbon dioxide is heavier than air.
What You'll Need: cardboard tube from a roll of wrapping paper; knife; candle; candleholder; matches; glass; baking soda; measuring spoon; vinegar

Caution: *This project requires adult supervision.*

Cut a 10-inch section of cardboard tube from a roll of wrapping paper. Put a candle in a candleholder in a safe place on a table. Light the candle. Put 1 teaspoon of baking soda into an empty glass. Add 1 inch of vinegar to the glass. You will see bubbles forming. These bubbles contain carbon dioxide gas, which is formed as the vinegar and baking soda mix together. Hold up the cardboard tube, and tip it down toward the candle flame, but don't get it too close or it will burn. Carefully pour the bubbles from the glass into the tube and toward the flame without getting liquid into the flame. Observe what the flame does.

What Happened? As you poured the bubbles into the tube, the carbon dioxide gas traveled down the tube and came out the other end, covering the flame and keeping oxygen from it. The flame went out.

SPINNING SNAKE

68

What You'll Learn: Warm air rises.

What You'll Need: paper plate; markers; scissors; thread

Draw an oval shape in the center of a lightweight paper plate. Starting at the oval, draw a spiral line around and around four or five times until it reaches the edge of the plate. Use a scissors to cut along the spiral line from the outside edge to the center oval. Draw eyes to make the center oval of the plate into a snake's head. Poke a small hole into the center of the head. Put a thread through the hole from the top, and tie a big knot in it so the thread will not pull through. Color the snake's body with stripes. Hang the snake by the thread above a heat source, such as a radiator or heating vent. Watch to see what your snake does.

What Happened? Heat from the heat source caused air to rise up toward your snake. As the air molecules bumped into you spiral-shaped snake, they caused it to spin around.

A TIGHT SQUEEZE

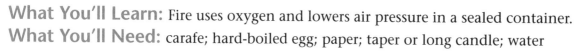

69

What You'll Learn: Fire uses oxygen and lowers air pressure in a sealed container.

What You'll Need: carafe; hard-boiled egg; paper; taper or long candle; water

Caution: *This project requires adult supervision.*

Find a bottle, such as a carafe, with a neck slightly smaller than a peeled egg. Peel the shell from a hard-boiled egg, and check to be sure that the egg just fits into the neck of the bottle and will not fall through.

Crumple up a piece of paper, and drop it inside the carafe. Use a taper or a long candle to light the paper at the bottom of the carafe. Quickly pop the egg into the neck of the bottle. Watch the egg get pulled into the bottle as the paper burns. Pour water into the bottle to extinguish the fire if necessary.

What Happened? As the paper burns, it uses up oxygen. Because the egg is sealing the neck of the bottle, no more air can get in to replace the oxygen. This reduces the air pressure in the carafe until the outer air pressure is strong enough to push the egg into the carafe.

MAKING A BAROMETER

70

What You'll Learn: A barometer is an instrument that measures air pressure.

What You'll Need: modeling clay; two rulers; water; large bowl; narrow, clear plastic bottle; string; pen and paper; tape

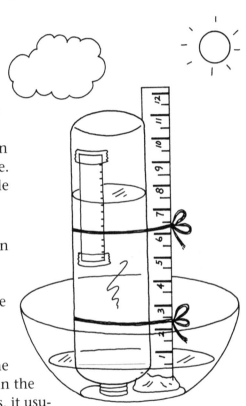

Stick the end of a ruler into a ball of modeling clay. Flatten the bottom of the clay so that it will hold the ruler upright on a table. Pour about 3 inches of water into a large bowl. Fill a narrow, clear plastic bottle three quarters of the way with water. Cover the opening of the bottle with your hand, turn the bottle upside down, and carefully lower the neck of the bottle into the bowl. When the opening of the bottle is beneath the water, remove your hand from the opening. Put the ruler on its clay stand into the bowl of water, and stand it right next to the bottle. Use two pieces of string to attach the bottle to the ruler so that the bottle will stand upright.

Take a piece of paper about 1 inch wide and 4 inches long, and put a mark every ¼ inch on the long side of the paper. Tape this paper scale on the plastic bottle so that about one third of the paper scale is above the water line in the bottle. Observe your barometer each morning and evening. By looking at your paper scale, you will see that the level of the water in the bottle changes from day to day.

What Happened? If air pressure rises, the air will press down more on the surface of the water in the bowl and raise the level of water in the bottle. If the air pressure falls, the air will press down less on the water in the bowl and lower the level of water in the bottle. When air pressure drops, it usually means that bad weather is approaching. Use your barometer to predict changes in the weather. Keep track of your predictions to see how well you do. You may need to add water to the bowl of your barometer occasionally, as some of it will evaporate.

UP AND DOWN

71

What You'll Learn: A gas will have a greater volume as its temperature increases and a lesser volume as its temperature decreases.

What You'll Need: balloon; pop bottle; bucket of ice water; bucket of hot water; clock

Fasten a balloon onto the neck of an empty soda pop bottle that has been sitting overnight and is at room temperature. Feel the bottle. It will be neither hot nor cold. Then put the bottle into a bucket of ice water, and leave it there for 15 minutes. Feel the bottle. It is cold. Now put the bottle into a bucket of hot water. The balloon inflates. If you put the bottle back into the ice water, the balloon will deflate.

What Happened? When you put the bottle in the hot water, you added heat energy to the air in the bottle. This made the air molecules move around more and spread out, so they took up more space. Some of the air went into the balloon and inflated it. When you put the bottle back into the ice water, you took heat energy away from the air in the bottle. This made the air molecules move less and take up less space, so the balloon deflated.

BALLOON IN A GLASS

72

What You'll Learn: Air presses in all directions.

What You'll Need: balloon; glass

Hold a balloon so that it dangles down into an empty glass. Hold the glass in one hand and the balloon in the other as you blow into the balloon. As you inflate the balloon, the part of the balloon trapped in the glass will swell out and touch the sides of the glass. Continue to blow. In a few more puffs, you can remove the hand holding the glass. You can lift the glass by holding the end of the balloon. The air pressure inside the balloon exerted force outward in all directions.

73 UNSPILLABLE WATER

What You'll Learn: Air pressure can be stronger than gravity.

What You'll Need: juice glass; water; 4×6-inch index card; sink

Fill a juice glass full of water. Let the water run over so that the rim of the glass is wet. Be sure that you fill the glass right up to the top. Place a 4×6-inch index card on top of the full glass of water. Be sure to press the card down securely with your hand so that it makes a good seal all around the wet lip of the glass. Working over a sink, hold the card in place with one hand as you turn over the glass. Carefully let go of the index card. The card will stay in place, and the water will stay in the glass.

What Happened? The force of air pressure against the card was stronger than the force of gravity on the water. The air pressure held the card in place.

 # WATER FOUNTAIN 74

What You'll Learn: Moving air has less pushing power than still air.

What You'll Need: tall glass; water; two drinking straws; scissors

Fill a tall glass with water. Stand one straw in the water so that the straw is about 1 inch above the top of the glass. If the straw is too long for your glass, cut it to the proper length with scissors. Place the glass on a table in front of a plant that you want to spray with water. Hold another straw at a right angle to the straw in the glass of water. The tip of the horizontal straw should just touch the tip of the upright straw. Blow hard through the horizontal straw, and you will create a spray for your plant.

What Happened? Normally, the air presses down on all the water in the glass with equal force, both inside and outside the straw. However, when you blow air over the straw, the moving air doesn't press down as hard as the still air over the rest of the water. That means that the air presses down harder on the water outside the straw and forces the water inside the straw up until it sprays out the top.

BOOK BLAST

75

What You'll Learn: Compressed air has great strength.
What You'll Need: books; large airtight plastic bag

Challenge a friend to move three books stacked on top of one another on a table by simply blowing at them. Your friend will be unable to move the books.

Now place a large plastic bag on the table, and put the three books on top of the bag. Leave the open end of the bag sticking out over the edge of the table. Hold the opening together, leaving a hole as small as possible. Blow into the bag. Take your time; stop to rest if you need to. If you blow long and hard enough, the books will rise off the table. They will be supported by the compressed air in the plastic bag.

ROCKET POWER

76

What You'll Learn: Compressed air has great strength.
What You'll Need: construction paper; scissors; tape; two drinking straws; modeling clay; empty bottle of dish-washing liquid

Caution: *Never launch your rocket at anyone.*

Cut a 3-inch square of construction paper diagonally so that you have two triangles. Fold each triangle in half, and tape the folded triangles to one end of a drinking straw so that they look like fins on a rocket. Cut 4 inches off the other end of the straw. With modeling clay, make a small pointed nose, and put it on the tip of the straw.

Cut a hole in the cap of a dish-washing liquid bottle large enough to push a second straw through. Put modeling clay around the straw to help seal up any gaps in the cap. Slip the rocket straw onto the straw that sticks out of the bottle cap. Point the nose of your rocket up in the air. Squeeze the plastic bottle to launch your rocket.

What Happened? When you squeezed the bottle, you forced air out of the bottle. The moving air went into the rocket and propelled it.

77 WIND SOCK

What You'll Learn: A wind sock tells you the direction and general strength of the wind.

What You'll Need: coffee-can lid; scissors; cloth; stapler or needle and thread; string; ribbon

Cut the inside from a coffee-can lid so that you are left with the rim. Put a 15×30-inch piece of cloth over the plastic rim, and secure it by stapling or sewing. The cloth will overlap about 1½ inches. When the cloth is secure around the rim, staple or sew the length of cloth so that you have a long sleeve. Punch three holes in the cloth around the rim. Thread a 15-inch piece of string through each hole, and tie each piece securely with a knot around the rim. Tie all three strings together about 5 inches in front of the rim. Then tie the ends of all three strings together to form a loop, which you'll use to hang your sock from a fence post or tree in the yard. Sew or staple three 1-foot strips of ribbon to the end of the sleeve. Hang the wind sock in an open area in your yard. The wind sock will tell you the direction of the wind. If there is no wind, the sock will hang down limp. If the wind is strong, the sleeve will stand straight out.

WIND VANE 78

What You'll Learn: A wind vane points into the wind.

What You'll Need: heavy cardboard; pencil; ruler; scissors; string; nut, bolt, or other weight

Draw a wind vane in the shape of an arrow onto a sheet of heavy cardboard. Your vane should be about 14 inches long and 2 inches wide, and the tail should be wider than the point. Cut the wind vane from the cardboard with scissors. Try to balance your cardboard wind vane on the point of a pencil, and mark the spot on the wind vane where it balances. Punch two holes into the wind vane at this balance spot; each hole should be ½ inch from the edge of the vane. Tie an 18-inch piece of string through the top hole and a 12-inch piece of string through the bottom hole. Tie a nut or bolt to the bottom piece of string for weight. Tie the top piece of string to a tree branch where the vane can swing easily without hitting anything. When the wind blows, your wind vane will point directly into the wind. The larger surface of the tail provides more resistance to the wind and causes the point to face into the wind.

PINWHEEL

79

What You'll Learn: Moving air molecules create a force that can cause a paper wheel to spin.

What You'll Need: ruler; paper; scissors; pencil with an eraser; pin

Measure and cut a piece of paper to make an 8-inch square. Use a ruler to draw a line from one corner of the square to the opposite corner through the middle of the paper, and then do the same for the other two corners. You have divided your square into four equal triangles. Put an X in the bottom left corner of each of the triangles. Cut from each corner along the lines you drew halfway to the center of the square of paper. Bend each corner that has an X in it to the center of the paper so that they all overlap, and then carefully put a straight pin through all four corners to hold them in place at the center of the paper. Put the point of the pin into the eraser on your pencil. You now have a simple pinwheel. You can swing the pinwheel, run with it, blow on it, or hold it in the wind. The moving air molecules will strike the paper and make it spin.

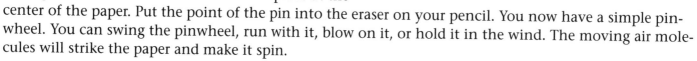

Flight and Air Pressure

Air has volume and mass, and just like any other thing with volume and mass, it can cause friction. The force created by this friction is called *air resistance*. Like all friction, air resistance pushes against an object in motion and slows it down. People sometimes harness the power of air pressure in different ways.

80 CLINGING CARD

What You'll Learn: You can use a low-pressure area to lift a card without touching it.

What You'll Need: index card; scissors; ruler; pencil; pin; empty spool of thread

Cut an index card into a 4-inch square. Mark the middle of the card. Put a pin into the middle of the card. Put a spool of thread over the pin so that the pin sticks up into the center of the spool.

Pick up the spool and card, holding the card against the bottom of the spool with your finger. Blow into the spool. Continue blowing, and slowly remove your finger from the card. If you are blowing hard enough, the card will not fall but will continue to stick to the empty spool.

What Happened? The moving air from your blowing created a low-pressure area between the card and the spool. Normal air pressure beneath it held the card in place.

OUT OF THE WIND 81

What You'll Learn: A stream of air will follow a curved surface.

What You'll Need: large plastic pop bottle; candle; candle-holder; matches

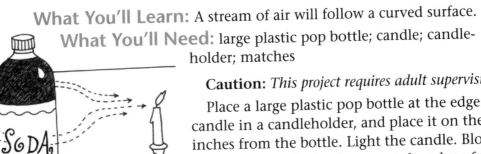

Caution: *This project requires adult supervision.*

Place a large plastic pop bottle at the edge of a table. Put a candle in a candleholder, and place it on the table a couple of inches from the bottle. Light the candle. Blow hard on the side of the bottle that is nearest the edge of the table. The moving air will follow the curve of the bottle around to the back and put out the burning candle.

BOOMERANG

82

What You'll Learn: A boomerang is an example of active flight.

What You'll Need: index card; pen; scissors

A paper airplane glides across the room making use of a condition we call passive flight. One of the earliest forms of active flight was the boomerang used by the Aborigines of Australia. You can make a simple boomerang that will work.

Draw your boomerang on an index card in a V-shape with the legs of the V open wide and each 2-inch leg looking like a long balloon. Cut out your boomerang, and balance it flat on two fingers of your left hand. Flick one of the legs with the forefinger of your right hand. It should take off like a little propeller and then return toward you.

WING IT

83

What You'll Learn: The shape of a wing gives it lift and allows an airplane to fly.

Daniel Bernoulli, a Swiss scientist, discovered in 1738 that moving air has less pushing power than still air. This idea, called Bernoulli's principle, is used in the design of airplanes.

To demonstrate the principle, cut a strip of paper 2 inches wide and about 8 inches long. Hold one corner of a 2-inch side of the strip in each hand, and hold it just below your lower lip. Gently blow across the strip of paper. You will see that the paper rises.

What Happened? The air you blow over the top of the paper is moving air, so it has less pushing power. The air pressure underneath the strip remains normal. The strong air pressure underneath pushes up and causes the strip of paper to lift. Wings of airplanes are shaped with curved tops to make the air move fast, and the fast-moving air along the top of the wing reduces air pressure and causes lift.

84 PAPER AIRPLANES

What You'll Learn: Shape is a factor in how well things fly through the air.

What You'll Need: paper; tape measure; pen

Throw a flat sheet of notebook paper as far as you can, and then measure the distance it traveled. Try several times, and write down the greatest distance it traveled. Now wad the sheet of paper into a ball. Throw it several times, and measure the distance it traveled each time. Write down the greatest distance it traveled.

Take another sheet of notebook paper. Fold it into an airplane, such as the one shown. Throw the airplane several times. Does it travel farther than the other sheets you threw? Experiment with different designs for your plane. Which works best?

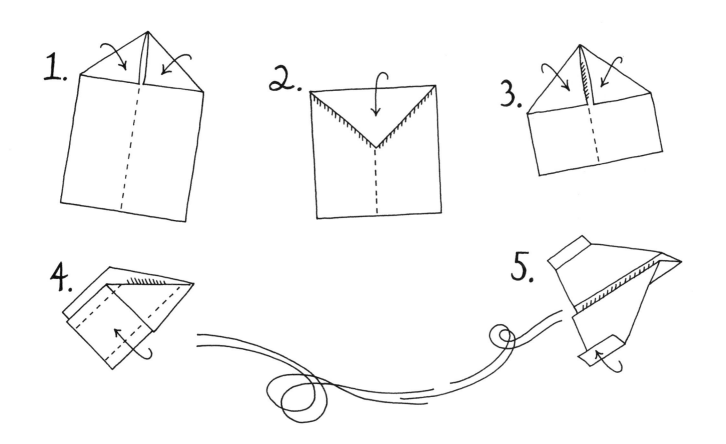

85 FAST AND SLOW LANDING

What You'll Learn: Compressed air under a parachute makes it fall more slowly.

What You'll Need: paper; ruler; scissors; small rock; tape; watch; thread

Cut an 8-inch square of paper. Tape a small rock to the middle of the paper. Wad the paper into a ball around the rock, and drop it from waist height off a staircase, porch, or deck. Ask a friend to use a watch with a second hand to time how long it takes the paper and rock to fall to the ground. Take the paper off the rock.

Tape a 10-inch piece of thread to each of the four corners of another 8-inch square of paper. Tape all four threads to the small rock. When you lift the paper up, it will look something like a parachute, and the rock will hang underneath the center. Drop the rock from the same place, and time the fall.

What Happened? When the paper was flat, it had a larger area than when it was crumpled into a ball. The paper ran into more air molecules on the way down, and the force of these additional air molecules slowed the paper and the rock as they fell.

86 PARACHUTE POWER

What You'll Learn: The more air trapped beneath a canopy, the slower a parachute will fall.

What You'll Need: paper; scissors; ruler; tape; string; paper clips

Cut two 12-inch squares and two 8-inch squares of paper. Securely tape 10-inch pieces of string to all four corners of all four pieces of paper. Gather the four strings from one square of paper, and tie them to a paper clip. Repeat for the other three squares.

Drop an 8-inch square and a 12-inch square of paper at the same time from a staircase, porch, or deck. Which reaches the ground last, the big or the small parachute? Add three more paper clips to the 8-inch parachutes. Drop both 8-inch parachutes. Which one reaches the ground first? Put a small hole in the middle of one 12-inch parachute. Drop both 12-inch parachutes. Which one reaches the ground first?

What Happened? You will find that the more surface area your parachute has, the slower it will fall. The larger surface encounters more air molecules as it falls, and so it falls slower. A parachute with a heavier load falls faster because the force of gravity working against the air resistance is greater.

 # SPINNERS

What You'll Learn: Air pressure can cause objects to move.

What You'll Need: 8-inch paper plate; ruler; pen; scissors

Hold an 8-inch paper plate in the palm of your hand so the plate is parallel to the floor. Drop the plate, and observe what happens. Use a ruler to draw three lines across the plate that divide it into six equal pieces. Cut a slit 2½ inches long on each line from the outside edge of the plate toward the middle. Make a triangular flap along the left side of each section by folding the plate upward at each slit. Drop the plate again, and observe it as it falls.

What Happened? The flaps caused your plate to spin as it fell the second time. Air molecules pushed against the surface of the flaps as the plate fell and made it spin.

88 GO FLY A KITE

What You'll Learn: Compressed air pushes a kite upward so that it can fly.

What You'll Need: two thin pieces of wood; measuring tape; marker; string; wrapping paper; scissors; tape; cloth

Get two thin pieces of wood, one 36 inches long and the other 18 inches long. Put a mark on the long stick 1 foot from one end. Using string, fasten the middle of the short stick to the long piece in a cross shape at the mark. When the two sticks are secured firmly in the middle, tie a piece of string from end to end of the four sticks to form a kite shape.

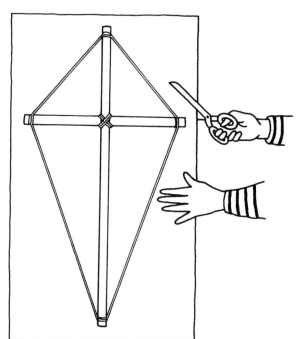

Cut a piece of wrapping paper that is 21 inches wide and 39 inches long. Lay the frame of your kite on the wrapping paper. Cut the paper in the shape of the kite, making it 1½ inches larger than the string outline on all sides. Fold the 1½ inches of paper over the string outline, and tape it securely all around.

Attach two 6-inch pieces of string to the long stick of the kite frame, one about 3 inches above the crossed sticks and one about 3 inches below the crossed sticks. Tie these two pieces of string together, and then tie them to the end of a ball of string. Tie a 6-foot piece of string to the tail end of the long stick. Tie strips of cloth at intervals along the string for a tail.

Take your kite outdoors in a large open area; make sure you're well away from any power lines or trees. As you fly your kite, pay attention to how the pressure of the air makes it move. Feel the power of the air pressure as it pulls on the string in your hand.

Water

Water is an important substance for life on Earth. Pure, ordinary water is made up of hydrogen and oxygen. When heated, water evaporates as gas. When cooled sufficiently, it freezes into a solid.

STRAINERS AND FILTERS

89

What You'll Learn: Strainers and filters separate bits of solid from a liquid.
What You'll Need: knife; orange; hand juicer; mesh strainer; two bowls; coffee filter

Caution: *This project requires adult supervision.*

Cut an orange in half with a knife. Use a hand juicer to squeeze out as much juice and pulp as you can from both halves of the orange. Hold a large mesh strainer over a bowl, and pour the juice and pulp into the strainer. Notice how quickly the liquid flows through the strainer. Check the strainer. It will probably contain seeds and large pieces of pulp. Rinse the strainer, and put a coffee filter in it. Now pour the juice through the filter into a second bowl. Notice that the juice flows more slowly through the filter. Look at the filter in the strainer. Did it catch more pieces of pulp?

What Happened? The coffee filter trapped material that the metal strainer did not. If you look at the strainer, you can see that it has small holes in it that allow liquids and small particles to pass through but not larger particles. The coffee filter works in the same way, but its holes are so small you can't see them. Smaller holes mean that it will trap smaller particles.

A FILTER AT WORK

90

What You'll Learn: A filter can remove suspended substances from liquids.
What You'll Need: water; measuring cup; four glasses; sand; measuring spoon; sugar; milk; cocoa; spoon; coffee filters

Pour 1 cup of water into each of two clean glasses. Add 1 tablespoon of sand to one glass. Add 1 tablespoon of sugar to the second glass. Pour ¼ cup of milk into a third glass, and add 1 teaspoon of cocoa. Using a clean spoon each time, thoroughly stir the liquids. Place a coffee filter into the top of a clear glass. Hold the edges of the filter over the rim of the glass so that the filter does not slip inside. Slowly pour the sand mixture into the filter. Does the filter catch the sand? Rinse out the glass. Pour the sugar mixture into the glass through a clean filter. Does the filter catch the sugar? Dip your finger into the filtered water, and taste it. Is it sweet? Rinse out the glass. Pour the milk and cocoa mixture into the glass through a clean filter. Does the filter catch some of the cocoa? Your filters will catch some of the suspended substances but won't filter out substances that have been fully dissolved.

FILTERING OUT DIRT

91

What You'll Learn: You can filter suspended matter from water by using a wick.
What You'll Need: cardboard box; two bowls; water; dirt; wool yarn

Set an 8-inch-tall cardboard box on a table. Set a bowl of clean water on top of the box. Gently drop a small handful of dirt into the water. Much of the dirt will remain suspended in the water, and the water in the bowl will be discolored.

Set an empty bowl on the table right next to the cardboard box. Twist together several 1-foot strands of wool yarn to make a rope. Put one end of this rope, or wick, into the bottom of the bowl of dirty water. Put the other end of the wick down into the empty bowl. After a while, drops of clear water will drip off of the free end of the wick into the empty bowl.

What Happened? The material in your rope absorbs water and draws it from the bowl. It leaves the dirt behind, however, so the water that drips into the second bowl is clean.

OVER THE TOP

92

What You'll Learn: Water expands when it freezes.

Fill a clean, plastic margarine tub with water. Make sure that the water level comes right up to the brim of the tub. Carefully place the tub of water into the freezing compartment of your refrigerator. Be very careful not to spill the water as you move the tub. The next day, remove the tub of water. Look at it carefully. The ice in the tub will be above the brim. The water will be over the top because water expands when it freezes.

Sinking and Floating

Objects that are more dense than water will sink in water. Objects that are less dense will float. Whether or not an object floats depends on the material it is made of and on how much space it occupies.

FLOAT OR SINK

93

What You'll Learn: Some objects will float in water while others sink.

What You'll Need: bathtub of water; pen and paper; various household items, such as a paper clip, a lemon, a small sheet of aluminum foil, a plastic fork, a key, a wooden block, a cork, a strip of cloth, and a pencil

Fill a bathtub with water. Gather up various objects from around the house to test, and make a list of all the objects on a piece of paper. Next to the name of each object, write "FLOAT" or "SINK" depending on what you think it will do. One by one, put the objects in the tub of water. Does the object float or sink? Were any of your predictions wrong? Did some objects, like the piece of foil, float or sink depending on how they were shaped?

SINKING SAILORS

94

What You'll Learn: Paper sinks faster in soapy water than in plain water.

What You'll Need: scissors; newspaper; ruler; dish-washing liquid; two large glasses; water

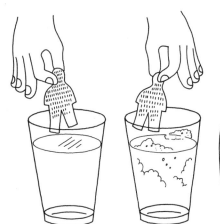

Fold a piece of newspaper in half, and cut two identical human figures from it. The two "sailors" that you cut from the paper should be about 2 inches at their widest point and about 4 inches tall. Fill two glasses with water, and put some dish-washing liquid into one of the glasses. Hold each of the sailors above a glass of water. Drop them at the same time. Both will sink, but which will sink faster?

What Happened? The sailor in the soapy water gets wet first and sinks faster because soap weakens the attraction between the water molecules.

95 UP PERISCOPE

What You'll Learn: Air weighs less than water and can be used to make an object float.

What You'll Need: plastic bottle with a narrow neck; scissors; four quarters; plastic tubing; modeling clay; bathtub filled with water

Cut two small holes, one above the other, in the side of a plastic bottle, such as an empty shampoo bottle. With adhesive tape, firmly attach two quarters on either side of both holes. Put a piece of plastic tubing like the kind that is used in aquariums into the neck of the bottle. Securely seal the opening of the bottle around the tubing with modeling clay.

Lower your submarine into a bathtub of water, keeping one end of the tubing above water. Hold your sub under the water until it fills up with water and sinks. Now blow through the end of the plastic tubing. As you blow, you will force air into the submarine and force water out the holes. As the submarine fills with air, it will rise to the surface. By blowing in or releasing air through the tubing, you can cause your submarine to rise or sink.

What Happened? Air weighs less than water. When your submarine is filled with water, it is more dense and it sinks. When it is filled with air, it is less dense and it floats. Real submarines move up and down in the water in the same way.

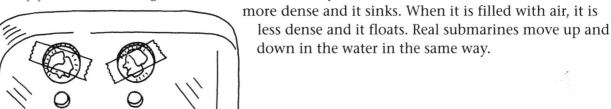

LIGHT AND SOUND SHOW

Light and sound both travel in waves. Light is a wave of energy, and the different colors of light have different levels of energy. Sound waves travel as vibrations through the air, and different levels of vibration produce different sounds. Light waves travel in a straight line, but sound waves spread out in all directions. Both light and sound can be either reflected or absorbed by materials they run into. Light waves can also be refracted, or bent, when they run into certain substances, such as water.

Spectrum of Colors

Sunlight contains all the colors of the rainbow blended together to make white light. These colors are red, orange, yellow, green, blue, indigo, and violet. But when sunlight shines on different things, not all colors are reflected equally. Some things, like grass, appear green to us because only the green light is reflected to our eyes; the rest of the colors are absorbed by the grass. Colors are only visible when light shines on objects.

96 RAINBOWS EVERYWHERE

What You'll Learn: Water drops can bend white light and break it into different colors.

Be on the watch for rainbows. The fine spray made by lawn sprinklers, mist from waterfalls, and the sun shining on a layer of rain can all cause rainbows. How many colors can you see in a rainbow? If you are lucky enough to see the sun reflect on two layers of rain, you may see a double rainbow!

 # MAKE YOUR OWN RAINBOW 97

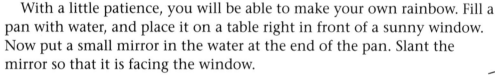

What You'll Learn: Light looks white, but it is really made up of rainbow colors.
What You'll Need: shallow pan; water; mirror; white paper

With a little patience, you will be able to make your own rainbow. Fill a pan with water, and place it on a table right in front of a sunny window. Now put a small mirror in the water at the end of the pan. Slant the mirror so that it is facing the window.

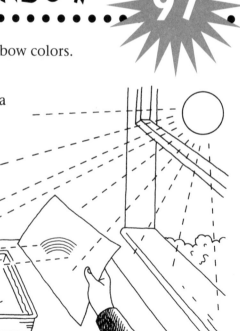

Next, hold a sheet of white paper between the window and the pan of water. Slowly tilt the mirror back and forth to catch the light at different angles as it passes through the water and hits the mirror. The light will reflect from the mirror and pass through the water. As it passes through the water, it will bend. If you angle the mirror in just the right way, the light will bend enough to make a rainbow that will show up on the paper. Be patient and keep trying; sometimes it can take a while.

PRISMS

98

What You'll Learn: White light is composed of all the rainbow colors.

What You'll Need: cardboard; scissors; prism; white paper

Cut a slit in a large piece of cardboard. Place the cardboard in a sunny window so that a shaft of sunlight shines through the slit. In one hand, hold a prism in front of the cardboard so that the sunlight passes through it. With your other hand, hold a sheet of white paper so that the light passing through the prism shines on it. You will see a rainbow of colors on the paper.

CHANGING COLORS

99

What You'll Learn: Color filters let through light of the same color as themselves, and they block other colors.

What You'll Need: cardboard; scissors; ruler; cellophane in red, blue, green, yellow, and orange; tape; markers; white paper

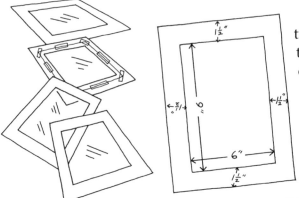

Take five pieces of 9×12-inch cardboard, and cut out the centers, leaving a frame that is 1½ inches wide all around. Using tape, securely fasten one sheet of colored cellophane to each cardboard frame. These frames now hold five color filters.

Look through one of the filters. What does it do to the colors of objects in the room? Try another. Look through two filters at a time. What do you see? Draw simple pictures or shapes on several pieces of white paper, using only one color of marker for each piece of paper. View each picture through a filter that is the same color as the picture. What do you see? Look at the pictures through filters of different colors. Continue to experiment with your filters.

100 MIXING LIGHTS

What You'll Learn: You can mix colored light to produce new colors.

What You'll Need: 12-inch square box; scissors; ruler; a cord with a plug at one end and a socket at the other; lightbulb; black paper; red, blue, and green cellophane; tape; white paper; mirrors

Cut a few holes in the top of a 12-inch square box to let out heat. Cut a square 3 inches wide and 5 inches high in one side of the box; the bottom of the square should be 1 inch above the bottom of the box. Cut a hole in the other end of the box big enough for a lightbulb to go through. Put the socket through the hole and into the box, and screw the lightbulb into the socket.

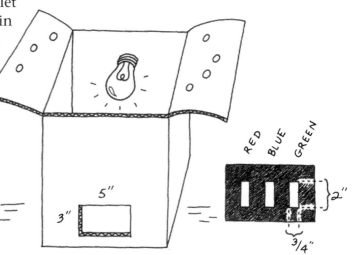

Cut out a 4×6-inch piece of black paper; cut three vertical rectangles that are each 2 inches tall and ¾ inches wide in the black paper. Tape a strip of red cellophane over the leftmost hole; tape a strip of blue cellophane over the center hole; tape a strip of green cellophane over the rightmost hole. Tape the black paper with the color filters over the square you cut in the side of the box. Put a sheet of white paper on the table in front of the filters.

Plug in the light cord, and then turn out the lights in the room. The light from your box will shine through the filters onto the white paper, showing red, blue, and green light. Use a mirror to reflect the red light onto the green light. What color do you create? Now reflect the blue light onto the green light. What color do you create? What other colors can you mix to form new colors?

COLOR MIX-UP

101

What You'll Learn: The colors of the spectrum produce white light when mixed together.

What You'll Need: three flashlights; cellophane in red, blue, and yellow; rubber bands; white paper

Cover the lens of a flashlight with red cellophane, and hold the cellophane in place with a rubber band. Cover the lens of a second flashlight with blue cellophane, and hold it in place with a rubber band. Cover the lens of a third flashlight with yellow cellophane, and secure it with a rubber band.

Set a sheet of white paper on the floor. Darken the room. Shine the red flashlight on the paper, and you will see a red spot. Shine the blue flashlight on the paper, and you'll see a blue spot. The yellow flashlight will produce a yellow spot.

Now overlap the spots of light from the yellow and blue flashlights; you will see a green spot. Ask a friend to shine the red light on your green spot, and the light will be almost white.

A COLORFUL SPINNER

102

Cut a 4-inch circle from a piece of cardboard. Mark the middle with a pencil, and then divide the circle into three equal sections. Color one section red, one blue, and one yellow. Using the pencil, poke a hole on either side of the center point ½ inch from the center. One hole should be in the red section, and one hole should be in the blue section.

Thread a 3-foot piece of string through one hole and back through the other. Tie the two ends of the string together. Slip two fingers of each hand through the loops in the ends of the string. Twirl the spinner around about a dozen times until the string is twisted.

Pull your hands apart firmly, and the string will start to unwind, making the spinner twist rapidly. When your hands are apart and the string is unwound, the momentum will cause the string to twist the other way. Move your hands toward each other to let the string twist. Repeat these motions over and over. If you time them right, you can get the spinner moving quickly. Look at the colored side of the spinner. What color do you see? The primary colors mix to form other colors.

NOT JUST BLACK AND WHITE

What You'll Learn: Different colors will be seen when you view spinning black-and-white circles.

What You'll Need: white paper; pencil; ruler; scissors; black paper; glue; marker; tape; knitting needle; paper plate

Draw and cut out three circles of white paper that are each 5½ inches in diameter. Put a small hole in the center of each circle. Draw and cut out a circle of black paper that is 5½ inches in diameter. Cut the black circle in half. Cut one of the halves in half.

Use these materials to make several different disks. Glue a black half-circle onto a white circle so that the disk is half black and half white. Glue a black quarter-circle onto a white circle so that the disk is one-quarter black and three-quarters white. Using a black marker, divide one white disk into eight pie-wedge shapes. Color some of the pie wedges black, leaving others white.

Wrap some tape around the middle of a knitting needle. Put the knitting needle through the middle of a 6-inch paper plate, and push the plate down to rest on the tape. Spin the plate. Be sure it spins smoothly and doesn't wobble. Use this as your spinner. Poke the knitting needle through the hole in the center of one disk, and let the disk rest on the paper plate. Spin the plate, and look at the disk as it spins. What colors do you see? Do you see different colors when the disk is spinning quickly or slowly? Spin the other disks to see what colors they produce.

COLORS AT A DISTANCE

104

Ask a friend to tie narrow strips of different-colored cloth to the bottom of a coat hanger so that the strips hang down neatly. Have your friend hang the coat hanger on a tree limb some distance from you.

Divide a sheet of paper into two columns. Write your name at the top of one column and your friend's name at the top of the other column. Down the left side, list the colors of your strips of cloth: yellow, orange, red, green, blue, black, and so on. When your friend says that the coat hanger is ready to be viewed, carry the sheet of paper and your pen, and walk toward the strips of cloth. As soon as you can see a color, write the number "1" on the paper under your name and next to the color you see to indicate that you saw that color first. Continue numbering all the colors as you see them. Now let your friend have a turn. Do you both agree on which color you were able to see first? Try the experiment again at a different time of day when the light is different. Compare your results to your first experiment.

BLACK TO COLORS

105

Take a white paper towel, and cut a strip 2 inches wide. Tape the strip to a pencil, and lay the pencil across the rim of a glass so the paper towel hangs into the glass. Cut the paper towel so that the bottom of it just touches the bottom of the glass as it hangs from the pencil. Draw a ¼-inch stripe on the paper towel about 1½ inches from the loose end with a black felt-tip marker.

Pour 1 inch of rubbing alcohol into the glass. Set the pencil on top of the glass so that the towel is in the alcohol and the black ink line is above the alcohol. Let the materials sit for an hour, looking at them now and then. Do you see any colors besides black on the paper towel?

What Happened? The color in the marker's ink was created by combining several other colors. As the alcohol was absorbed by the paper towel and traveled upward, it took some of the ink with it. It carried the different colors different distances, so they appeared in layers on the paper towel above the black line.

PLANT DYES

106

What You'll Learn: You can makes dyes of primary and secondary colors from plants.
What You'll Need: cloth; laundry marking pen; pen and paper; knife; beet; saucepan; water; stove; strainer; container; clothes hanger; clothespins; carrot; onion; tea; coffee; blueberries

Caution: *This project requires adult supervision. These dyes can stain your clothes or other materials.*

Number several squares of cloth with a laundry marking pen. Write the numbers in a column on a sheet of paper. Carefully chop a beet into tiny pieces. Put a small amount of water in a saucepan, and drop the chopped beets into the water. Boil for an hour, adding a little water to replace any that boils away. Strain the liquid into a container. Pour the strained liquid back into the saucepan, and drop the cloth labeled "1" into it. Boil for 15 minutes. Carefully remove the cloth. Hang it with a clothespin on a clothes hanger outdoors to dry. Write "BEETS" next to the "1" on your paper. Repeat this process with a carrot, onion skins, tea, coffee, and blueberries. When you're finished, compare the colors of the cloth pieces.

MIXING PIGMENTS

107

What You'll Learn: By mixing primary colors, you can produce new colors.
What You'll Need: watercolors; paintbrush; jar of water; white saucer; paper

Dip a paintbrush into a jar of water and then into blue watercolor paint. Drop some of this blue paint onto a white saucer. Rinse your brush in the water. Pick up some yellow watercolor paint on the brush, and drop some of this onto the blue paint on your saucer. Use your brush to mix these two colors. You will have a shade of green. Rinse the paintbrush. In the same way, combine red and yellow to make orange on another spot on the saucer. Rinse the paintbrush again, and combine red and blue to create violet. Now, use your primary colors and the new colors you created to paint a picture.

Light and Heat

Light is a form of energy. Heat is also a form of energy.
Sometimes an energy source will produce light and heat at the same time.
Sometimes the energy in light can be used to produce heat.

MEASURING HEAT FROM SUNLIGHT

108

What You'll Learn: An object exposed to sunlight will become hotter than a similar object in the shade.

Put cardboard in front of a window to block the light from part of the windowsill. Set two thermometers that are indicating the same temperature on the windowsill. Be sure that one thermometer is in direct sunlight and the other is in the shade you created by putting cardboard in the window. Wait 15 minutes, and then check the temperatures on the thermometers.

What Happened? Some of the energy in the sunlight was converted to heat when it struck the thermometer. That heat raised the temperature reading on the thermometer. The other thermometer was not exposed to sunlight, so it registered a lower temperature.

109 BULB IN A BOX

What You'll Learn: A lighted bulb gives off heat.

What You'll Need: shoe box; scissors; cord with a plug at one end and a socket at the other; 60-watt lightbulb; a thermometer; clock; paper and pen

Cut a hole in one end of a shoe box, and put the lightbulb socket into the box through the hole. Screw a 60-watt lightbulb into the socket, but don't turn it on yet. Place a thermometer inside the shoe box, and put the lid on the box. After 15 minutes, read the temperature inside the shoe box, and write it down.

Put the thermometer back in the box. Turn on the lightbulb. Be sure that the bulb is lit and is not touching the thermometer. Put the lid on the box. After 15 minutes, turn off the lightbulb. Being careful not to touch the hot lightbulb, read the temperature inside the box, and write it down. Compare the two temperatures.

What Happened? The lightbulb generates both light and heat. The heat from the bulb raised the temperature of the air in the shoe box, so the thermometer had a higher reading the second time.

BURNERS ON A STOVE 110

What You'll Learn: Some energy sources produce both light and heat.

Caution: *This project requires adult supervision.*

One evening when the electric burners of your kitchen stove are off and the stove is not in use, ask permission to use it for a brief experiment involving light and heat.

First, look at the burner carefully. It will not be giving off any light. Hold your hand about 9 inches above the burner. You will not feel any heat.

Turn on the burner, and wait about five minutes. Turn off the kitchen lights. Look at the burner. It is glowing, giving off light as well as heat. Turn on the lights. Turn off the burner. Hold your hand about 9 inches above the burner. You will be able to feel the heat.

MAKING SUN TEA

Usually when people want to make tea, they put a tea kettle on the stove and bring water to a boil. Then they put tea in the boiling water and use the energy of the hot water to release flavor from the tea. Sunlight also produces enough energy to brew a tasty batch of tea.

Place a large jug of water outside in full sunlight. Drop four tea bags into it, and screw the lid onto the jug. Wait for several hours while the sunlight heats the water. Watch often to see what is happening. When it's ready, enjoy the tea!

BURNING SUN

What You'll Learn: By focusing the sun's light, you can create a spot of great heat.

What You'll Need: paper; magnifying glass; glass of water

Caution: *This project requires adult supervision.*

On a clear, sunny day, place a sheet of white paper on a concrete or asphalt surface. Hold a magnifying glass a few inches above the paper, and you will see a spot of light on the paper. Move the magnifying glass around to get the smallest spot of light possible on the paper. Hold the glass in this position, and watch the paper. In a short time, the focused light will burn a hole in the paper. When you're done, pour some water on the paper to make sure it's no longer burning. Be careful! Don't focus light on your skin or clothing or anything else that might burn.

Opaque, Transparent, Translucent

We can say that an object is opaque, transparent, or translucent.
If it is *opaque*, it will not let any light pass through. *Transparent* objects
transmit light; we can see through them. *Translucent* objects pass light,
but they diffuse it so that objects cannot be clearly distinguished.

 ## SEE-THROUGH SHIRT

113

If you hold a T-shirt out at arm's length in front of you and try to look through the T-shirt to see a wall behind it, you will be unable to see the wall. The T-shirt blocks the light, so it appears to be opaque.

Now pull the T-shirt down over your head, and try to look through it. You will be able to see the wall. When your eyes are close enough to the T-shirt, the shirt is translucent. Although the view is less clear, you can still see through the shirt. Try this with other materials, such as a towel, a handkerchief, a scarf, a tablecloth, or a sweater.

SHADOW CLOCK

What You'll Learn: When rays of light are blocked by an object, a shadow is produced.

What You'll Need: chalk; watch or clock

On a sunny morning, draw an arrow with chalk on your patio or driveway. Ask a friend to stand facing in the direction of the arrow with one foot on either side of the arrow. Now trace around your friend's shadow with chalk. Is it a long or short shadow? Is it in front of your friend or behind your friend? Inside the shadow, write down the time.

Every two hours, ask your friend to come back and stand in the same spot. Each time, trace around your friend's shadow, and write the time inside this shadow.

At the end of the day, look at the shadow tracings. Why are some shadows in front of where your friend stood and some behind? Why are some shadows small and some long?

PROJECTING IMAGES

What You'll Learn: Water can be changed from transparent to translucent to opaque.

What You'll Need: 5-gallon aquarium; water; stiff white paper; tape measure; slide and slide projector; milk; measuring cup; eyedropper; large spoon

Fill a 5-gallon aquarium two thirds of the way with water. Prop up a sheet of stiff white paper about 65 inches behind the aquarium. Put a slide in a slide projector, set the projector on the table in front of the aquarium, and project the slide through the water and onto the sheet of white paper. You will need to focus the projector, and you may need to move the sheet of paper to get a good, sharp image.

Measure out 1 cup of milk. Using an eyedropper, put three drops of milk into the aquarium, and stir. Now look at the image on the paper. It will be blurred because the milk and water mixture doesn't permit as much light to pass through. Now mix in the remainder of the milk. Does any light pass through?

SHADOW PUPPETS

What You'll Learn: When rays of light are blocked by an object, a shadow is formed. The nearer the object is to the light, the bigger the shadow is.

What You'll Need: paper; scissors; pencil; wooden sticks; tape; cassette and cassette recorder; sheet; two flashlights

With a couple of friends, plan a shadow puppet show to share with family or other friends. Cut puppet shapes out of construction paper. For Halloween, for example, you might cut out the shape of a witch, a cat, a ghost, and so on. To do a woodland story, you might cut out simple shapes of a deer, rabbit, bird, and squirrel. Tape each of your puppet shapes onto a thin stick of wood so that they will be easy to hold.

Plan the story you are going to tell, and record it into a tape recorder. You can include background music if you want. Drape a sheet over a doorway. When it is show time, the audience will sit on one side of the door while the puppeteers sit on the other side. Turn on the tape. While two friends shine flashlights at the drape, operate the stick puppets in front of the flashlights. The audience will see the shadows of the puppets on the sheet in the doorway.

THROUGH THE DRINKING GLASS

What You'll Learn: Water can be changed from transparent to translucent to opaque.

What You'll Need: magazine; scissors; glass; water; bowl; cornstarch; spoon

Cut a small, interesting picture from a page of a magazine. Fill a clear glass halfway with water. Place the glass on top of the picture that you have cut from the magazine. Look down into the glass through the water. You will be able to clearly see the picture because the water is transparent. In a bowl, mix a little cornstarch with water. Put a little of the cornstarch mixture into the glass of water above the picture. The water is no longer clear and transparent. This solution is translucent; you will still be able to see the magazine picture, but the picture will be partially obscured. Add the rest of the cornstarch mixture. The water in the glass will become opaque; you will no longer be able to see the picture through the water.

Reflection and Refraction

Most objects are visible because they reflect light, or cause light to bounce off of them. Reflections can fool you; if you look in a mirror and wink your left eye, it appears that the right eye of the image in the mirror is winking. Light can also be refracted. This means that its path bends as it passes through a substance because the substance makes it travel at a different speed.

 ## HOT, HOTTER, HOTTEST

What You'll Learn: Objects reflect light differently depending on what color they are and what material they are made of.

What You'll Need: four resealable plastic storage bags; water; white, orange, and black construction paper; aluminum foil; thermometer; pen and paper

Fill four resealable plastic storage bags with water, and seal them tightly. Place the bags outside in a sunny spot on the sidewalk, driveway, or patio where they will not be disturbed. Wrap one bag in a sheet of white construction paper, one in a sheet of orange construction paper, one in a sheet of black construction paper, and one in a sheet of aluminum foil. Predict what effect the different wrappings will have on how the sun's energy heats the water in each bag. Which will be the warmest? Which will be the coolest? Using a thermometer, measure the temperature of the water in each bag after an hour. Were your predictions correct?

119 A KALEIDOSCOPE

What You'll Learn: Mirrors reflect multiple images off of one another.

What You'll Need: three small mirrors of the same size; tape; waxed paper; pencil; scissors; construction paper

To make a kaleidoscope, tape together three small mirrors in a triangle shape with the mirror-sides facing inward. Stand the mirrors up on a piece of waxed paper, and trace around the bottom of the mirrors. Cut out this triangle shape, and then tape the piece of waxed paper in place at the bottom of the three mirrors. Cut out many small pieces and shapes from colored sheets of construction paper, and drop them inside the mirrors. Give your kaleidoscope a shake, then look inside. You will see some interesting patterns. The mirrors will reflect interesting shapes and colors.

120 SPLIT PERSONALITY

What You'll Learn: A mirror reverses images from left to right.

What You'll Need: magazine; scissors; white paper; glue; mirror

Cut a picture of a person's face from a magazine. Cut the picture in half vertically, and glue the left half of the face onto a sheet of white paper. Now place the paper flat on a table. Hold a mirror in the middle of the paper so that the mirror touches the line where you cut the picture in half. Look at the picture and the image in the mirror. You will see what appears to be a complete face again.

ON AND ON AND ON

121

What You'll Learn: Mirrors can be placed to create multiple reflections.

Stand with your back to a large wall mirror in good light. Hold a large hand mirror up in front of you, just below eye level, in front of your nose. Look at the reflection in the mirror. You may need to adjust the position of the hand mirror, but you will soon see a reflection in the mirror that is multiplied many times. How many reflections can you count?

MIRROR WRITING

122

Prop a mirror upright on a table, and set a piece of paper on the table so it can be clearly seen in the mirror. Try to write a short message to a friend on the paper, but don't look at the sheet of paper on the table. Instead, look at the paper's reflection in the mirror. This will not be easy to do; it may take several practice tries. After you've written your message, your friend can hold it up in front of a mirror and easily read what you wrote.

PEEKABOO

What You'll Learn: The path followed by light rays is reversible.

What You'll Need: clay; two small mirrors; white paper; pencil; black construction paper; ruler; scissors; lamp; protractor

Using a lump of clay to help hold it in place, set a small mirror on the center of one edge of a sheet of white paper. Draw a line on the paper to show the front edge of the mirror.

Take a sheet of 9×12-inch black paper. Mark the middle of the paper. Fold back a flap at each end that is 3×9 inches. Cut a ¹⁄₁₆-inch slit from the middle of the 12-inch side of the paper to within 1 inch of the top of the paper. Stand this black paper shield, using the flaps to help hold it up, on the end of the white paper opposite the mirror, a little to the right of center. Set a lamp about 3 yards behind the black shield so that the light will shine through the slit.

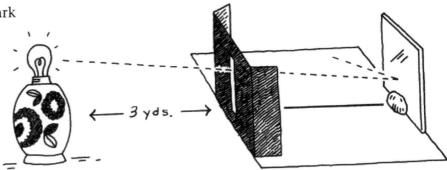

Turn on the lamp, and turn off the other lights in the room. The light shining through the slit in the shield will make a narrow beam on the sheet of white paper. Draw lines on the white paper that trace the path of the light beam both before and after it strikes the mirror. With a protractor, measure the angle between the mirror and the incoming beam of light, and then measure the angle between the mirror and the beam of reflected light. How do they compare?

Now set a second mirror on the white paper so it is in the path of the reflected beam of light. What does it do to the reflected light? Turn the mirror slightly from side to side to make the light reflect back along the same path it was following.

What Happened? The light traveled toward the first mirror at a fixed angle, and the mirror reflected the light at exactly that same angle but in a different direction. The second mirror did the same thing. However, when you changed the position of the second mirror by moving it from side to side, you caused the light to strike it at a different angle. This changed the path of the light reflected by the second mirror.

124 PINHOLE CAMERA

What You'll Learn: The image in a pinhole camera is upside down.

What You'll Need: oatmeal box; scissors; aluminum foil; tape; needle; tissue paper

Cut a 1-inch square in the bottom of an empty oatmeal box. Tape a piece of aluminum foil over the 1-inch square. Prick a hole in the middle of the aluminum foil using a fine needle. Tape a piece of tissue paper over the open end of the oatmeal box. On a bright, sunny day, point the box at a house or tree across the street. Look through your pinhole camera. You will be able to see an image of the house or tree on the piece of tissue paper, but the image will be upside down.

Producing Sounds

The sounds we hear are caused by vibrations. When the vibrations reach your ear, they cause your eardrums to vibrate, and your brain perceives the vibrations as sound. Things sound different to us when they vibrate at different rates.

125 BOUNCING CEREAL

What You'll Learn: Sound waves are vibrations, and they travel through the air.

What You'll Need: plastic wrap; metal bowl; rubber band; cereal flakes; cookie sheet; spoon

Stretch a piece of plastic wrap tightly over the top of a metal bowl. Secure it in place with a tight rubber band. Put a small handful of cereal flakes on top of the plastic wrap. Stand near the bowl, and loudly bang a cookie sheet with a spoon. Watch the cereal flakes.

What Happened? Striking the cookie sheet produced sound waves—vibrations—that traveled through the air. When the vibrations struck the plastic wrap, it vibrated, too, and that caused the cereal to move.

FRYING PAN CHIMES 126

What You'll Learn: Sound waves can be passed from one object to another and amplified.

What You'll Need: string; scissors; tape; frying pan; knife; dinner fork; salad fork; soup spoon; teaspoon

Cut five pieces of string, each about 15 inches long. Tie the end of a piece of string just beneath the tines of a dinner fork. Tape the string inside a frying pan, on the side directly opposite the handle. Repeat this process with the salad fork, knife, soup spoon, and teaspoon. When you hold the frying pan by its handle, the silverware will dangle down on strings and bang into one another. Shake the pan, and listen to the sound it produces.

What Happened? When the silverware pieces struck each other, they vibrated. The vibrations from each piece traveled up the strings at the same time and caused the pan to vibrate. The large pan amplified the combined vibrations and produced pleasant sounds.

SYMPATHETIC VIBRATIONS

127

What You'll Learn: Vibrations produce sound and can transfer from one object to another.

What You'll Need: two identical wine glasses; water; pencil; short piece of fine wire

Pour water into a wine glass until it is one third of the way full. Tap the side with a pencil. It will make a musical sound. By adding more or less water, you can change the sound. The tapping causes the side of the glass to vibrate.

Pour exactly the same amount of water into a second wine glass. When you tap both glasses with a pencil, they will give the same sound. If there is a difference in the sound, add a little water to one glass until they do make the same sound. Stand the water glasses on a table about 4 inches apart. Place a piece of fine wire across the top of the glass that is farthest from you. Strike the closest glass, and watch the wire on the other glass. It will move slightly. The wire responds to your tapping on the other glass because the glasses vibrate in sympathy. If you continue to tap, the wire on the far glass will gradually move enough to fall.

 # BOTTLE MUSIC

128

Stand eight empty bottles side by side on a table in front of you. Fill the bottle on the left about a quarter of the way full with water. Add water to the next bottle so that the water level is a bit higher than in the first bottle. Continue adding water to the bottles so that each one has a little bit more water in it than the bottle on its left. Blow across the bottle on the left, and you'll hear a low note. Blow across the bottle on the right, and you'll hear a high note. By adjusting the amount of water in each bottle, you can produce a whole musical scale.

What Happened? When you blow across the bottle, you cause the air inside to vibrate, which produces a sound. The amount of air in the bottle affects the sound it makes. The bottles with more air produce low sounds, and the bottles with less air produce high sounds.

RUBBER BANDS

What You'll Learn: The rate that something vibrates determines the sound that it makes.

What You'll Need: cardboard box; three long rubber bands

Stretch three rubber bands around a small, sturdy cardboard box that is about 8 inches square and 2 inches deep. Space the rubber bands about 2 inches apart.

Pluck each of the rubber bands. Do they make a sound? Do they sound alike? Pull the middle rubber band tighter, and tie a knot to shorten it a little. Pull one of the other rubber bands very tight, and tie a knot to shorten it. Pluck the rubber bands again. Which one produces the highest sound? Which one produces the lowest sound?

What Happened? By pulling the rubber bands tighter, you changed the rate at which they vibrate. The change in vibration rate caused a change in the sound they made.

TEA KETTLE SOUNDS

Caution: *This project requires adult supervision.*

Bring water to a boil in a tea kettle. Listen to the whistling sound the kettle makes. Whistle a note of the same pitch, imitating the sound of the kettle as closely as you can. You will hear only one sound. Now whistle a note that is higher than the sound of the tea kettle. Listen closely as you whistle. Instead of hearing two sounds, you will hear three!

If the kettle's note has 500 vibrations a second, and you whistle higher at a note of 600 vibrations a second, the third low note you hear is the difference between the first two, or a note that is 100 vibrations a second. The source of the extra note is the motion of the air particles in the waves of sound.

131 A KAZOO

What You'll Learn: Vibrating air against paper will make a musical sound.

What You'll Need: tube from a roll of paper towels; waxed paper; rubber band; pen

Stretch a 4-inch square of waxed paper over one end of a cardboard tube from a roll of paper towels. Put a rubber band around the tube to hold the waxed paper in place. Use a pen point to poke a hole in the tube about 1½ inches from the covered end of the tube. Now hold the open end of the tube to your mouth, and hum a tune into it. The waxed paper will vibrate and hum your tune along with you.

FISH LINE MUSIC 132

What You'll Learn: The rate that something vibrates determines the sound that it makes.

What You'll Need: smooth board; pencil; ruler; hammer; ten 1-inch nails; scissors; nylon fishing line

Lay a 16×6×1-inch board flat on the table in front of you so that one of the 6-inch sides is nearest you. Draw five straight pencil lines down the length of the board about 1 inch apart, beginning 1 inch down from the top and 1 inch in from the left side. Pound a nail about ½ inch deep at the top of each line.

Cut five pieces of nylon fishing line in the following lengths: 14, 12, 10, 8, and 6 inches. Tie a loose slip knot in both ends of each piece of fishing line. Put the slip knot of the 14-inch piece of fishing line over the top left nail on your board, and pull it tight. Put the slip knot at the other end of the fishing line over a loose nail, and stretch the line as tightly as you can toward the bottom of the leftmost pencil line that you drew. Hammer the nail into the board about ½ inch deep. Nail the other pieces of fishing line onto the board in the same way. Work from left to right on the board, each time using the longest piece of fishing line that you have left.

You now have a musical instrument. Pluck each string with your index finger. Which string has the highest sound? Which has the lowest? Practice with your new instrument, and use it to make music.

133 ANIMAL SOUNDS

What You'll Learn: By varying vibrations, you can create animal sounds.

What You'll Need: 1-quart milk carton; scissors; string; paper towel; water

Cut through a 1-quart milk carton 4 inches from the bottom. Using scissors, punch a small hole in the center of the bottom of the carton, and thread the end of a 24-inch piece of strong string through the hole. Tie several knots to make a large knot that will not pull through the hole.

Wet a paper towel, squeezing out the excess water. Hold the milk carton in one hand, and put the wet paper towel around the string about 10 inches from the carton. Give the wet towel a quick pull while pressing it with your fingers. It will make a squawking noise that is amplified by the milk carton.

By varying how much string you leave between the wet towel and the box, you will be able to produce sounds resembling a rooster's crow and a lion's roar.

BULL ROARER

134

What You'll Learn: An object in motion can cause sound waves.

What You'll Need: wooden paint stirrer; drill; string

Caution: *This project requires adult supervision.*

Take a wooden paint stirrer, and drill a hole about ½ inch from the end of the handle. (If you do not have a paint stirrer, any thin strip of wood about 1 foot long will work.) Securely tie a piece of sturdy string through the hole in the stick. Find a place where you can safely twirl the stick; be sure that no people or objects are in your way. Rapidly twirl the stick around in front of you in a circle. It will make a big roar of sound. As the stick moves through the air, it begins to spin, then it catches the air and causes air molecules to vibrate. The vibrating air molecules produce the sound you hear.

Sound Waves

When sound travels through the air, it causes the air molecules to vibrate back and forth at a regular rate. Sound waves can also travel through other mediums including liquids, such as water, and solids, such as metal, by making the molecules of water or metal vibrate back and forth. Sound waves travel different distances and at different speeds through different mediums. Sound waves are reflected if the vibrations bounce off of an object, and they are absorbed if the vibrations are stopped by an object.

SOUND WAVE MODEL

135

What You'll Learn: Particles of air vibrate backward and forward but do not travel with sound.

What You'll Need: thread; scissors; six glass marbles; tape; clothes hanger

Cut six pieces of thread, each 10 inches long, and attach one end of each thread to a glass marble using tape. Now tie the other end of each thread to the horizontal piece of a clothes hanger, leaving about 1 inch between each thread that you tie.

Hang the hook of the clothes hanger from a shower-curtain rod. Pull back one of the end marbles. Let the marble go so that it strikes the next marble. Watch what happens. It hits the second marble, which swings to the side and hits the third marble, and so on.

Sound travels through the air in the same way. A vibration causes one molecule of air to move from side to side and bump into another molecule, which then moves from side to side at the same rate and bumps into a third molecule, and so on.

REFLECTING SOUND

What You'll Learn: Sound can be reflected.
What You'll Need: two umbrellas; two pieces of sturdy bendable wire; a watch that ticks loudly; tape

Lay two open umbrellas on the ground so that the handles face each other about 2 yards apart. Twist the middle of a piece of sturdy bendable wire around the handle of one umbrella. Push both ends of the wire into the ground to support the umbrella so that it is horizontal with the ground. Repeat with the other umbrella.

Move a ticking watch along the handle of one umbrella to find the spot where the ticking sounds loudest. Tape the watch in place at that spot. Now move to the other umbrella, and hold your ear to the corresponding spot on the umbrella handle. You should be able to hear the watch.

What Happened? The sound of the watch strikes the inside of the umbrella it's attached to and bounces off of it. The sound waves then strike the inside of the other umbrella and bounce off at the same angle. The shape of the umbrella focuses the sound waves at a single point along the handle.

SOLIDS AND SOUND

What You'll Learn: Solid objects carry sound vibrations and make them louder.
What You'll Need: metal bowl; water; scissors; fork; table

Fill a metal bowl with water. Take a pair of scissors, and cut the air. Listen to the sound. Now submerge the scissors in the bowl of water, and open and close the scissors while you hold your ear to the metal bowl. Does it sound different?

Hit the tines of a fork against the edge of a table, and listen to the sound. Then hit the tines of a fork against the edge of a table, and quickly touch the end of the fork handle to the table. Is the sound louder?

Do sound waves sound the same to you when they travel through the air as they do when they travel through other mediums?

TICK TICK TICK

138

What You'll Learn: A balloon containing carbon dioxide will amplify sound waves.
What You'll Need: baking soda; measuring spoon; bottle; vinegar; balloon; ticking clock

Put 2 tablespoons of baking soda into a narrow-necked bottle. Add 3 tablespoons of vinegar. Pull the opening of a balloon down over the neck of the bottle so that it fits tightly. The balloon will become filled with carbon dioxide gas produced by the baking soda and vinegar.

Hold up a ticking clock about 1 foot from your ear. You will be able to hear the ticking sound. Now, hold the inflated balloon up to your ear with one hand while you hold the ticking clock on the other side of the balloon about 1 foot away. The ticking of the clock will now be much more distinct. The balloon filled with carbon dioxide acts as a kind of lens that focuses the sound wave.

SOUND PATH

139

What You'll Learn: Sound waves can travel through a piece of thread.
What You'll Need: thread; two forks; three spoons

Tie a fork to the middle of a 30-inch piece of thread. Hold the free ends of the thread to your ears. Lean forward from the waist so that the fork hangs freely and does not touch you or your clothing. Have a friend hold a fork and a spoon and strike them while you listen. You will hear a soft sound. Now ask your friend to strike the fork hanging from your neck with a spoon. The noise will travel along the thread, and you will hear it quite loudly. Now tie a spoon to the thread on either side of the fork. Again hold the free ends of the thread to your ears. Ask a friend to strike the spoons and the fork with another spoon. You will hear a series of bell-like tones.

140 A SIMPLE TELEPHONE

What You'll Learn:
Sound travels through string better than it travels through the air.

What You'll Need: pen, nail, or other pointed object; two hard-plastic containers (such as cottage cheese containers); string

Use a pen to punch a small hole in the middle of the bottom of each of two hard-plastic containers, such as cottage cheese containers. Thread one end of a 12-foot piece of string through the hole in each container so that the end is inside the container. Tie knots in each end so that the string will not pull out through the hole.

Hold one cup, and give the other to a friend. Walk far enough apart so that the string between the cups is pulled tight. The string should not be touching anything in

the middle. Ask your friend to hold the cup over one ear while you whisper into the other cup. Your voice will make the string vibrate. The vibration will travel along the string to the other cup, and your friend will clearly hear what you whispered. Now listen while your friend whispers. Build other phones that use different lengths of string and different kinds of containers, and compare how well they work.

MAY THE FORCE BE WITH YOU

Any kind of push or pull on an object is a force. We see examples of this every day in moving cars, falling leaves, spinning tops, and in other familiar sights. The same forces that cause the movements we see every day also govern how planets move and how galaxies form. They play a big part in everything that happens everywhere in the universe, from a pin dropping to a star exploding. When we study force, we look at where different forces come from, how they are applied, and how they affect the movement of objects.

Gravity

Gravity is the attraction between physical objects. You see gravity at work any time you see an object fall to the ground. All objects exert gravity; the sun, the Earth, you, and a single strand of your hair all draw other objects toward them to some degree. However, gravity is only noticeable when it's very strong.

141 TIDES COME AND GO

What You'll Learn: The pull of the moon's gravity as it travels around the Earth causes a regular movement of the oceans, which we call the tides.

If you've ever spent the day at the ocean, you may have noticed that the water level at the shore changed throughout the day. The water creeped up the beach steadily and then gradually slipped out again. This rise and fall of ocean waters is called the tide. The moon causes the tide by the gravitational pull it exerts as it travels around the Earth every day.

If you ever spend the day by the ocean, pay attention to the changes in the tide as they occur. Or check weather reports in a local newspaper or other source to see what that day's tides were like. Check for several days in a row, or check one day each week for several weeks. Keep track of the tides over time to see how they change.

JOURNEY TO THE CENTER OF GRAVITY 142

What You'll Learn: The center of gravity is the point in an object where all of the weight is centered.

What You'll Need: paper clip; notebook paper; pencil; tape

Bend a paper clip open to make an L-shape. Put the tip of the short side of the paper clip on the tip of your index finger, and try to balance it. The paper clip will fall off. Take a half sheet of notebook paper, and roll it into a small tube around a pencil. Use tape at both ends of the paper to keep the tube from unrolling. Remove the pencil. Tape the end of the long side of the paper clip to the end of the tube of paper. Now try to balance the paper clip on your index finger.

What Happened? By adding more weight to the bottom of the paper clip, you changed the paper clip's center of gravity—the point where the force of gravity is equal on either side. That allowed you to balance the clip on your finger in a way that you couldn't do before.

LIFT AN ADULT

143

The Earth's gravity exerts a force on you that keeps you planted on the ground. An adult may be able to overcome that force by exerting an upward force to lift you in the air. But chances are very good that you cannot exert enough upward force to lift your mother or father off the ground—unless you use a lever.

Take a plank about 6 feet long, 1 inch or more thick, and 6 to 12 inches wide. Put a block of wood about 1 foot tall and at least as wide as the plank under the plank about 1 foot from the end. Lift up the long end of the plank until the shorter end touches the floor. Ask your mother or father to stand on the short end. When you step on the long end of the lever, your body weight will exert a downward force on one end of the plank, which will exert enough upward force on the other end to overcome gravity and lift your parent off the ground. If it doesn't work at first, move the block closer to the end of the plank where your parent is standing.

Laws of Gravity

Gravity may be a very powerful force, but it does have to obey some rules. For instance, the more mass an object has (or the heavier it is), the greater that object's gravitational pull. Gravitational pull is also affected by distance; as two objects get closer to each other, the pull between them increases. These basic rules are always true, for every object in every situation. By understanding these and other laws of gravity, we can better understand the world around us.

144 GRAVITY AND MASS

What You'll Learn: The strength of gravity depends on the mass of the objects that are attracting each other.

One of Isaac Newton's discoveries was that the strength of gravity depends on the mass of the objects attracting one another. Therefore, the same object would weigh less on the moon than on Earth, because the moon, being smaller than Earth, would attract that object less strongly. You cannot change the size of the Earth or easily travel to the moon, but you can very easily illustrate Newton's principle by changing the mass of a handy object here on Earth.

Weigh a five-pound sack of sugar. Pour about half of it out into a bowl. Weigh the sack again. Of course the sack now weighs about half of what it did originally. This obvious fact illustrates the important truth that half the mass is attracted by the Earth with half the force.

FALLING MARBLES 145

What You'll Learn: Heavy and light objects fall at the same speed.

What You'll Need: 15 marbles; two resealable plastic bags

Put five marbles in one plastic bag, and seal it. Put ten marbles in another plastic bag, and seal it. Raise both bags of marbles above your head as high as you can. Release the bags at exactly the same time, and drop them onto a carpet. Listen for the moment that they strike the floor, and you'll know that they landed at the same time.

What Happened? One bag obviously weighed more than the other, so you might have expected it to fall faster. The force that makes objects fall on Earth, though, is the gravitational attraction of the Earth itself. As with any object, the strength of the Earth's gravitational pull is determined by the Earth's mass. Since the Earth's mass is always the same, it exerts the same pull on any two objects that are the same distance from it.

146 HIGH BOUNCE

Collect some different balls (tennis ball, beach ball, softball, rubber ball, football, basketball, golf ball, etc.). Make a graph that has the names of the different balls across the bottom and height in feet along the sides.

Test the different balls to see which one bounces best on a concrete floor, porch, or driveway. Drop them one at a time from the same height in front of a large sheet of cardboard, and mark on the cardboard how high each one bounced. Measure each bounce, and indicate it on your graph.

What Happened? All the balls gained the same amount of energy when they fell. When they struck the ground, the downward force from gravity was converted into upward force that worked against gravity to send the ball up in the air. The different materials and sizes of the balls affected how well each one could convert the energy into upward force, and that affected how high each ball bounced.

TWO THUDS OR ONE? 147

What You'll Learn: Gravity exerts the same force on a moving object as it does on a stationary object.

What You'll Need: grooved ruler; wooden board; nails; hammer; block of wood; two marbles

Lay a grooved ruler on a wooden board about 1 inch thick, 6 inches wide, and 1 foot long. Hammer broad-headed nails close to one end of the ruler, on either side, so that the broad nail heads hold the ruler firmly to the board at one end. Wedge a 3-inch wooden block under the other end of the ruler. Have a friend stand by ready to help. Let a marble roll down the groove of the ruler. This will launch the marble horizontally. At the exact moment the marble leaves the end of the ruler, have your friend drop a second marble from exactly the same height. Look and listen. Do both marbles reach the floor at the same time? If they do, you'll hear only one thud.

What Happened? Both marbles hit the ground at the same time, even though one was traveling horizontally and the other was not. Gravity exerted the same force over the two marbles, even though one of them was in motion.

148 TARGET PRACTICE

What You'll Learn: A moving object will keep moving at a constant speed as gravity pulls it down.

What You'll Need: black paper; ruler; scissors; bean bag; bicycle

Challenge a friend to target practice. From a sheet of black paper, cut out two black circles. Make a 1-inch-diameter circle and a 6-inch-diameter circle.

Take turns with your friend riding past the target on your bike and trying to drop a bean bag on the target as you go by without stopping. After several tries, you'll learn when to drop the bean bag. Do you drop it when you are directly over the target? When you and your friend can hit the 6-inch target, try the 1-inch target.

WATER PRESSURE GAUGE

149

What You'll Learn: Weight causes pressure that results in a stronger flow of water.

What You'll Need: pencil; ½-gallon milk container; tape; water; sink

Use a pencil point to poke three holes, one directly above the other, on one side of an empty ½-gallon milk container. One hole should be about 1 inch from the bottom of the container; the middle hole should be 3 inches above the first; and the third hole should be 3 inches above the middle hole.

Put a piece of tape down the side of the container to cover up the three holes. Fill the carton with water, and set it down in the sink. Pull off the piece of tape, and watch the water flow from the holes. You'll see that the water shoots out the greatest distance from the bottom hole and the least distance from the top hole. You'll also see that the water from each hole squirts less and less far as time passes.

What Happened? As gravity pulls down on the water, the water exerts a downward force that we call water pressure. The more water you have, the greater the amount of downward force it will produce. The force of water pressure that made the water squirt out of the holes was stronger at the bottom of the carton than at the top because the bottom had more water above it pressing down. That's why the water squirted farther from the bottom hole. As the water drained from the carton, the amount of water pressure decreased, and the water didn't squirt as far.

SIMPLE SIPHON

150

What You'll Learn: Gravity affects the flow of water.

What You'll Need: two large jars; 3-foot length of plastic tubing

Fill a jar halfway with water, and set it on a table. Set another jar next to the first one. Now put one end of a 3-foot piece of plastic tubing into the jar containing the water and the other end in the empty jar. Lift the jar with water up so it is level with your head. Does anything happen?

Now set the jar down, and take the tubing out of the empty jar. Put the tubing in your mouth, and suck up water until the tubing is filled with water. Hold your thumb over the end of the tubing to keep the water from running out, and carefully lift the jar containing the water up so it is level with your head. Put the tubing into the empty jar, and remove your thumb. Watch what the water does this time.

What Happened? The part of the tubing that ran between the two jars was much longer than the part that was in the jar containing the water; the longer section of tubing had more water in it than the other section, so the downward water pressure in the longer section of tubing was much greater. This greater water pressure was enough force to overcome the pull of gravity on the water in the jar, so the water was drawn up through the tubing.

Paths of Objects

The movement of objects can occur in a straight, curved, or irregular path.
The way that force is applied makes a difference in the path
that an object will follow.

151 PENDULUM PATTERNS

What You'll Learn: A pendulum swings in a specific pattern.
What You'll Need: two chairs; dark paper; broom; paper cup; string; tape; salt

Stand two chairs about 3 feet apart, and cover the area between the chairs with a large piece of dark paper. Lay a broom handle across the backs of the chairs. Poke a small hole in the bottom of a paper cup. Tape a 6-inch string to the paper cup on either side to form a handle. Tie the handle of the paper cup to a 3-foot piece of string, and then tie the string to the middle of the broom handle between the two chairs.

Hold your finger over the hole in the bottom of the paper cup, and fill the cup with salt. Then pull the cup toward one of the corners of the sheet of dark paper. Release both your finger and the cup. The cup will swing like a pendulum in a pattern, and you will be able to see the pattern it swings in by looking at the salt that drops onto the paper.

 # SWINGING TOGETHER 152

What You'll Learn: The motion of one swinging weight will transfer to another object.
What You'll Need: two chairs; string; two paper cups; six marbles

Place two chairs about 4 feet apart. Tie a string between the backs of the chairs. Punch two holes opposite one another in the lip of a paper cup. Thread a 4-inch string through the holes, and tie a knot to make a handle for the cup. Repeat this process with a second cup. Tie a 2-foot-long piece of string to the handle of each cup. Tie the free ends of the strings to the string stretched between the two chairs; tie the strings so they are about 1 foot apart. Put two marbles in each cup. Hold one cup to the side, and then release it. Watch as it begins to swing. What happens to the other cup? Put four marbles in one cup and two in the other. What happens if the heavy cup is put in motion first? The light cup?

GHOST WALK

153

What You'll Learn: Energy from a wound-up rubber band can make an object move along a path.

What You'll Need: rubber band; empty spool of thread; toothpick; tape; candle; knife; pencil; handkerchief

Thread a rubber band through an empty spool of thread. Slip half of a toothpick through the rubber band at one end, and use a piece of tape to tape the toothpick to the bottom of the spool. Slice a 1-inch-thick piece from a candle, and poke a small hole through the center of it. Thread the other end of the rubber band through the candle ring, and then put a pencil through the end of the rubber band. Set the spool on the table so the toothpick side is touching the table surface. Wind the pencil around several times, and hold it in place. Cover the spool with a white handkerchief, and then let it go. Watch your little ghost creep across the table.

WHIRLY-GIG

154

What You'll Learn: Centrifugal force causes spinning objects to move toward the outside of a circle.

What You'll Need: paper; string; tape; cardboard toilet paper tube

Take a half sheet of notebook paper, and wad it up into a small ball. Stick the end of a 2-foot piece of string into the ball of paper, and tape it to the paper. Thread the string through a cardboard tube from an empty roll of toilet paper. Wad a full sheet of paper into a tight ball. Stick the other end of the piece of string into the large ball of paper, and tape it to the paper. Let the small ball stick out of the tube about 5 inches at the top, while the large ball hangs down from the bottom. Grasp the tube in one hand, and move your hand in a small circular motion so that the small ball spins around the tube. Spin it faster and faster, and watch the large ball begin to rise. Continue moving your hand, and pull down on the large ball. Watch what happens to the speed of the small ball.

What Happened? Some of the energy you applied by moving your hand generated a centrifugal force that caused the small ball of paper to move outward in a circle and pull up on the large ball.

WATCH AN OUNCE LIFT A POUND

What You'll Learn: Centrifugal force increases with an increase in speed.

What You'll Need: fishing line; empty cotton spool; a 1-ounce object; a 1-pound rock

Thread a 5-foot piece of fishing line through an empty cotton spool. At one end, securely fasten a 1-ounce object that can be whirled about without danger. Fasten a 1-pound rock to the other end of the fishing line.

Grip the spool so that you are also holding the string beneath it. Let the heavy rock dangle down about 10 inches. Rotate the light object in a horizontal circle above your head. When the light object is spinning around fast, you can release your grip on the string below the spool. As you continue to spin the light object, you will see the heavy object begin to rise on the string that goes through the spool. (Be sure to use a strong line and fasten objects securely so that the objects don't fly off!)

What Happened? Some of the energy you used to spin the light object around generated a centrifugal force that caused the object to move in a circle. As you applied more energy, the centrifugal force became strong enough to lift the heavy object.

PATH OF A BALL

156

Take a small ball with a good bounce, and throw it straight at a smooth wall. Watch the ball carefully. If it hits the wall straight on, it will bounce straight back to you. Now move to the side so that you can throw the ball so that it hits the wall at an angle. Watch the ball carefully. It will not bounce back to you; instead it will bounce off the wall at an angle equal to the angle at which it struck the wall. Move to another spot where you can throw the ball so that it hits the wall at an even sharper angle. Again watch the path of the ball bounce. It will be equal to the sharp angle at which the ball struck the wall.

CATAPULT

157

What You'll Learn: When you move the fulcrum from the center toward one of the ends of a lever, you change the distance and speed at which the ends move.

What You'll Need: wooden block; ruler; eraser; pen and paper

Find a place to do this project where you're sure the eraser won't hit anything or anyone. Place a small wooden block on a table. Rest the center of a ruler on the block. Put a small eraser on one end of the ruler, and quickly push the opposite end down to the table. Notice that both ends of the ruler travel the same distance. Measure how far the eraser was thrown, and write it down.

This time, rest the ruler on the block so that the block is about 2 inches from one end of the ruler; one end will be up in the air and the other will rest on the table. Put the eraser on the end of the ruler that is resting on the table. Give a sharp blow to the other end of the ruler. Notice that the one end of the ruler moves several times farther than the other end. Measure the distance that the eraser was thrown this time, and compare it to the previous measurement.

What Happened? The block of wood was acting as a fulcrum that transferred the force from one end of the ruler to the other. The closer the fulcrum is to one end of the lever, the more force it will transfer to the other end.

Laws of Motion

Three basic rules govern how things move, or how they react when force is applied to them. First, a stationary object will stay in place and a moving object will keep moving until a force acts on it; this is called *inertia*. Second, the effect that force has on an object depends on the amount of force and the mass of the object. Third, applying force to an object results in an equal force being applied in the opposite direction.

158 STARTING AND STOPPING

What You'll Learn: Inertia means that an object in motion will keep moving until a force stops it.

Put three rocks in the back of a toy truck as cargo. Push the truck forward quickly so that it picks up momentum, and then stop it suddenly. Watch to see what the rocks do when the truck is stopped.

What Happened? The rocks in the back of the truck were in motion. When you applied force to the truck to stop it, the rocks continued moving inside the truck until they were stopped by hitting the side of the truck.

BREAKING THE STRING 159

What You'll Learn: Inertia means that an object at rest will remain at rest until a force makes it move.

Cut a 2-foot piece of thread, and tie one end securely around a 6×4×2-inch block of wood. Tie the other end to a secure horizontal pole (such as a shower curtain or a porch railing) so the block of wood hangs down from it. Cut another 2-foot piece of thread, and tie one end of it securely around the block of wood also. Let the other end hang down freely. Now gently pull down on the lower piece of thread. Continue to pull slowly and steadily, increasing pressure until the upper thread breaks.

Set up your experiment again. This time, instead of pulling slowly and steadily, give a sharp, powerful tug to the bottom thread. This time the bottom thread will snap.

What Happened? The block of wood was at rest. When you pulled down steadily with increasing force, you overcame the block's inertia, pulling it downward and causing it to pull on the top thread and break it. When you pulled down quickly, you did not generate enough force to overcome the block's inertia; all of the energy was applied to the lower thread, causing it to break.

PULLEY POWER

160

What You'll Learn: A pulley can be used to lift weight.

What You'll Need: empty 1-quart milk carton; marbles; scissors; string; metal coat hanger; wire cutters; empty spool of thread; dowel; books

Open the flaps of an empty 1-quart milk carton, and put 24 marbles inside. Close up the carton, and punch a hole through the top with a scissors. Push a 3-inch piece of strong string through the hole, and tie the string in a knot to form a loop. Take a coat hanger, and use wire cutters to carefully cut off the long straight piece on the bottom. (Save this to use in Using a Roller on page 109.) Bend the two short arms of the coat hanger through the hole in the center of a spool of thread until the ends of the arms touch each other. Put the hook of the coat hanger through the loop of string you tied to the milk carton.

Set a dowel on a table so it extends 6 inches over the side of the table; set some heavy books on top of the dowel to hold it in place. Place the milk carton on the floor beneath the dowel.

First lift the milk carton 6 inches off the floor by holding the carton by the flaps and pulling it up in your hands. Now tie one end of a 5-foot piece of string to the dowel. Pass the other end of the string under the spool of thread. Lift the carton of marbles about 6 inches off the floor by pulling the string 12 inches. The milk carton will feel only half as heavy as it did before; pulling the string twice the distance that you raise the carton means you need to exert only half the force to lift it.

161 USING A ROLLER

What You'll Learn: A roller can make work easier.

What You'll Need: books; ruler; thin metal rod (such as the bottom piece cut from a coat hanger with wire cutters); empty spool of thread; string; toy car; empty margarine tub; marbles; paper and pen; cardboard

Put two stacks of books, 9 inches apart, at the edge of a table. Each stack should be 9 inches tall and placed so that part of each stack of books sticks out over the edge of the table. Place a thin metal rod through an empty spool of thread, and rest the rod across the stack of books. Add a few more books to each stack to hold the rod in place. Tie a 2-foot piece of string to the front of a toy car. Put the car on the table beneath the rod, and put the other end of the piece of string up over the spool of thread.

Punch two holes opposite each other in the rim of an empty margarine tub. Tie an 8-inch piece of string through the holes to form a handle for the tub. Tie the other end of the string that is attached to the toy car to the handle of your tub.

Add marbles to the margarine tub, one at a time, until there is enough weight to lift the toy car 5 inches into the air. Empty the tub, and count the marbles. Write the number down.

Add a third stack of books, 5 inches high, between the other two stacks. Use a sturdy piece of cardboard to make a ramp between the top of the middle stack of books and the table. Put the toy car at the bottom of the ramp.

Put marbles, one by one, into the tub until there's enough weight to pull the toy car to the top of the ramp. Empty the tub, and count the marbles. Write the number down. Using a ramp to help, did it take more or less weight to lift the toy car?

BLAST OFF

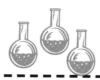

What You'll Learn: A force exerted in one direction creates an equal force in the opposite direction.

What You'll Need: two 3-foot dowels; hammer; fishing line; drinking straw; empty plastic screw-top bottle; vinegar; tape; baking soda; measuring spoon; tissue paper

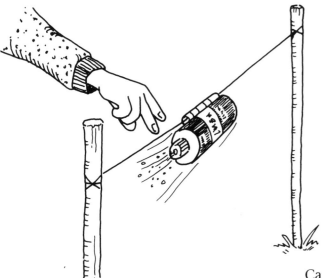

Carefully pound two 3-foot dowels into the ground about 6 feet apart. Tie a 7-foot piece of fishing line to one dowel, thread the loose end through a drinking straw, and then tie the other end to the second dowel, stretching the string tightly between the dowels.

Put a hole through the cap of an empty plastic screw-top bottle, such as a shampoo bottle. Remove the cap from the bottle. Pour an inch of vinegar into the bottle. Tape the bottle to the straw on the fishing line so the bottle is horizontal. Slide the bottle along the fishing line all the way to one end so that the cap is next to the dowel.

Put 3 teaspoons of baking soda into a small piece of tissue paper. Roll the paper up, slip it into the bottle, and quickly screw the cap back on the bottle.

Carefully shake the bottle back and forth for a few seconds, and then let go of the bottle. The bottle will travel the length of the fishing line, propelled like a rocket.

What Happened? The baking soda and vinegar produced carbon dioxide gas when they were mixed together. The gas was forced out of the hole in the bottle cap. As the gas pushed backward out of the bottle, it exerted an equal force in the opposite direction, which propelled the bottle forward.

163 WATER-POWERED BOAT

What You'll Learn: A force exerted in one direction creates an equal force in the opposite direction.

What You'll Need: knife; empty 1-quart milk carton; pencil; paper cup; bendable drinking straw

Carefully cut an empty 1-quart milk carton in half lengthwise. You only need one half, so set the other half aside. Set your half down on the table so you can see the inside of the carton. The top of the milk carton will be the prow, or front, of your boat, and the bottom will be the stern, or the back. Using a pencil, make a hole just big enough for a drinking straw to fit, near the bottom and in the center of the boat's stern.

Poke a hole of the same size in the side of a paper cup ½-inch up from the bottom. Bend a bendable drinking straw into an L-shape. Put the long end of the straw through the hole in the boat's stern. Now put the short end of the straw through the hole in the cup, and set the cup inside the boat.

Fill your bathtub or sink with water, and put the boat in it. Be sure that the straw poking out from the boat is below the water's surface. Hold a finger

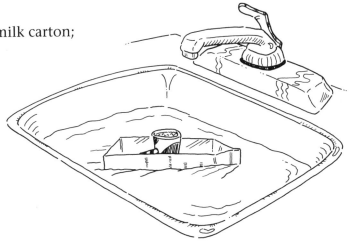

over the end of the straw in the paper cup while you fill the cup with water. Take your finger off the straw, and watch your boat sail.

What Happened? Gravity made the water flow out of the cup, through the straw, and into the sink. As it was forced out of the straw, the water exerted an equal force in the opposite direction, which propelled the boat forward.

ROLLING OATS RACE

164

What You'll Learn: Force is needed to overcome inertia.

What You'll Need: four identical metal washers; two empty oatmeal boxes with lids; tape; marker; cardboard; chair

Tape a heavy metal washer to the inside of an empty oatmeal box halfway between the top and bottom. Tape a second washer directly across from the first one, and put the lid back on the box. Take the lid off of a second oatmeal box. Tape a heavy metal washer to the underside of the lid, directly in the center. Put a washer inside the box, and tape it to the bottom, directly in the center. Put the lid back on the box. Put a mark on the lid of this box so you can tell the two boxes apart.

Arrange a large sheet of sturdy cardboard so one end rests on the seat of a chair and the opposite end rests on the floor. Use this ramp as a raceway for your two oatmeal boxes. Hold them at the top of the ramp, one in each hand, and release them at exactly the same time. Which one reaches the bottom first? Race them down the ramp several times. Does the same one always win?

What Happened? The box with the washers taped to the sides was always slower than the other one. As the slow box rolled, the washers on the side moved in a circular path. As the fast box rolled, the washers on the top and bottom stayed in one place. Gravity exerted an equal force on the two boxes, but some of that force had to be used to overcome the inertia of the washers in the slow box. More of the force was available to make the fast box roll, so it rolled faster.

Magnets and Metal

Magnetism is a property of the molecules of certain substances, such as iron, that will attract or repel other magnetized objects. In a magnet, the molecules line up in a way that creates a force. When a magnet is free to turn, it can be used to indicate the direction of the Earth's magnetism. The end of a magnet that points to Earth's North Pole is called the north pole of the magnet; the end that points to the Earth's South Pole is called the south pole of the magnet.

KEEP YOUR DISTANCE

165

What You'll Learn: Depending on which poles are brought together, magnets will either attract or repel each other.

What You'll Need: pencil; six doughnut-shaped magnets

Hold a pencil upright like a flagpole with your hand at the bottom. Put six doughnut-shaped magnets on the pencil, being sure to reverse every other one so that they will repel (push away from) each other. Now move the pencil into a horizontal position. What happens to the magnets?

MAKE A COMPASS

166

What You'll Learn: A magnet that can turn freely will align itself with Earth's magnetic field and point north.

What You'll Need: large tub of water; bar magnet; clean styrofoam meat tray; scissors

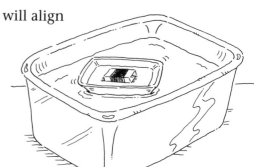

Set a big tub of water on a wooden table. Place a bar magnet in the middle of a small piece of styrofoam that you have cut from a clean meat tray. Set the styrofoam on top of the water in the middle of the big tub. Be sure that there is no metal in the area.

Allow the tray to float freely so that it can find its own direction. The tray will turn until one end of the magnet points north. The magnet is acting like a compass needle.

STRONG ATTRACTION

167

What You'll Learn: Only objects containing iron are attracted to magnets.

What You'll Need: horseshoe magnet; various household items, such as a paper clip, nail, hairpin, thumbtack, plastic spoon, wooden block, table tennis ball, toy car, penny, dime, aluminum foil, pop can, tin can, knife blade, cup, fork, belt buckle, etc.

Gather up many small objects from around the house, and make a guess as to whether or not they contain iron. Then test them to find out. Hold an object to the ends of a horseshoe magnet. If the object contains iron, it will be attracted to the magnet. If it does not contain iron, it will not be attracted. How often did you guess correctly?

168 MAGNETS AND RUST

What You'll Learn: Magnets can lose some of their magnetism.

What You'll Need: horseshoe magnet; a can of small nails; paper and pen; jar of water

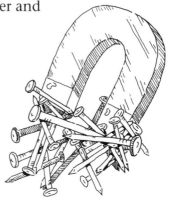

Many things can weaken a magnet. They can be spoiled by being repeatedly banged so that molecules are jarred and disarranged, for instance. In this experiment, you'll find out if rust weakens a magnet.

Dip a shiny horseshoe magnet into a can of small nails. Count how many nails it attracts. Repeat this three times, counting the number of nails attracted each time and taking the average. Then put the magnet in a jar of water, and leave it there until its surface is rusted. Then repeat your test of the magnet with the can of nails. Does the rust have any effect on the magnet's strength?

AN ELECTROMAGNET 169

What You'll Learn: Electricity can produce magnetism.

What You'll Need: iron bolt; electrical wire; 6-volt battery with screw-down terminals; various household objects

Caution: *Wires can become hot during this activity.*

Wind a 3-foot piece of electrical wire around a long iron bolt about 20 times; make the loops close together, and leave about 10 inches of wire loose on each side of the coil. Connect the two loose ends of the wire to a 6-volt battery. The bolt is now an electromagnet and will attract metal containing iron. Test the electromagnet using paper clips, spoons, and other household items to see how strong it is. Disconnect the wire from the battery, and see if the magnet still works.

What Happened? As electricity from the battery flowed through the wire, it caused the molecules in the bolt to align themselves in a way that created a magnetic force, and the bolt became a magnet.

MAGNET MERRY-GO-ROUND

170

What You'll Learn: A turning magnet will pull steel objects in a circle.

What You'll Need: two small magnets; an old record player; tape; thumbtacks; thin cardboard

Tape two small magnets to the turntable of an old record player. Turn on the record player. Place several thumbtacks on a sheet of thin cardboard. Hold the cardboard above the turntable. Slowly lower the sheet of cardboard over the turntable until you almost touch it. The magnetism will be exerted through the cardboard and will pull the thumbtacks around and around as the magnets spin on the turntable.

Lines of Force

The force of magnetism extends out from a magnet in all directions to form an area we call the *field* of the magnet. Objects affected by magnetism will feel the force of a magnet if they pass into its field. The field takes the shape of lines extending from the magnet, which we call *lines of force.*

171 HORSESHOE FIELD

What You'll Learn: Magnets create lines of force that form a magnetic field.

What You'll Need: horseshoe magnet; paper; iron filings

Place a horseshoe magnet on a table, and cover it with a sheet of thin paper. Sprinkle iron filings on the paper. Observe the pattern that the iron filings make as they are attracted to the magnet. This pattern gives you an idea of the shape of the field generated by the magnet. The filings show you a two-dimensional version of the field; the real field extends out from the magnet in all directions.

Check around your house to see if you have other magnets, such as round or square ones stuck to the side or front of your refrigerator. Experiment with these in the same way to see what patterns they make.

MAGNET OUTLINES 172

What You'll Learn: Magnets exert their force on objects that move into their field.

What You'll Need: two bar magnets; paper; iron filings

Place two bar magnets on a table. Put them with unlike poles facing each other, about 1 inch apart; unlike poles attract each other. Cover the magnets with a sheet of thin paper. Sprinkle some iron filings onto the paper. Observe the pattern that the iron filings make. The filings show you a two-dimensional version of the field generated by each magnet. Looking at the shape of the fields, you can see how the two magnets affect each other at the points where their fields meet.

Repeat this experiment, but this time set the magnets on the table with like poles facing each other, about 1 inch apart. Like poles repel each other. The lines of force from each magnet will appear to be different at the point where they intersect.

DISPERSING MAGNETISM

173

What You'll Learn: The force of magnetism cannot be exerted through steel.

What You'll Need: weak magnet; paper clip; aluminum cake pan; plastic; cardboard; steel cookie sheet

A magnet will attract a steel paper clip through many different objects. Hold the magnet under an aluminum cake pan. Put a paper clip in the pan; there is a strong attraction. By moving the magnet, you can move the paper clip all around the pan. Do the same test, putting a piece of plastic and then a piece of cardboard between the magnet and the paper clip. Again, there is a strong attraction, and you can move the clip.

Now put the paper clip on a steel cookie sheet. Put the magnet underneath. Instead of passing right through the sheet, the magnetism is dispersed. Depending on the strength of the magnet, either there will be no attraction or the attraction will be much weaker than it was through the other objects.

RIGHT THROUGH THE GLASS

174

What You'll Learn: The force of magnetism can be exerted through glass.

What You'll Need: metal objects, such as thumbtacks, nails, paper clips, etc.; bar magnet; glass jar

Set several small metal objects on the table. Move a bar magnet across the table toward one of the metal objects. When the magnet is close enough to the object, it will cause the object to move toward it. Try this with several of the objects.

Now take all of the metal objects that were attracted to the bar magnet, and drop them into a glass jar. Hold the bar magnet to the outside bottom of the jar. Put your hand across the mouth of the jar, and turn it upside down while holding the magnet in place at the bottom. Remove your hand from the jar opening. The metal objects don't fall. The magnetism passes through the glass and attracts the objects, holding them in place. If you remove the magnet, the objects will fall.

175 MAGNET MAZE

What You'll Learn: The force of magnetism can be exerted through paper.

What You'll Need: paper plate; pencil; bar magnet; paper clip; timer

Draw an interesting maze with lots of twists and turns and some dead-ends on the surface of a large, white paper plate. Make the path of your maze slightly wider than the width of a paper clip. When the maze is finished, ask a friend to hold the plate. Place a paper clip at the start of the maze. Holding a bar magnet beneath the paper plate, try to guide the paper clip through the maze without touching any of the lines. If the paper clip crosses a line, change places, and let your friend try to guide the clip through the maze. You might want to time yourselves to see how long it takes to move through the maze.

Transferring Magnetism

It is possible to transfer magnetism from a magnet to another iron or steel object. When this is done, the object to which the magnetism has been transferred will behave like a magnet for a period of time.

CHECKING MAGNETIC POLES

What You'll Learn: Opposite poles of a magnet attract.

What You'll Need: thread; tape; strong bar magnet; marker; large sewing needle; iron nail

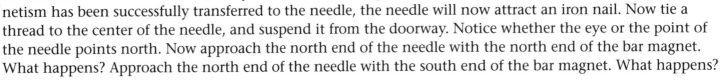

Tape a fine piece of thread to a doorway that is not near metal objects. Tie the loose end of the thread around the middle of a bar magnet. Let the magnet hang freely. The magnet will slowly align itself with the Earth's magnetic field, and one end will point north. Mark that end of your magnet with an N.

Now hold a large sewing needle by the eye, and stroke it repeatedly with the bar magnet toward the point. Always stroke it in the same direction, and hold the magnet away from the needle when you are moving it back to the eye of the needle. After two dozen strokes, test your needle. Is it magnetized? If the magnetism has been successfully transferred to the needle, the needle will now attract an iron nail. Now tie a thread to the center of the needle, and suspend it from the doorway. Notice whether the eye or the point of the needle points north. Now approach the north end of the needle with the north end of the bar magnet. What happens? Approach the north end of the needle with the south end of the bar magnet. What happens?

What Happened? By rubbing the needle with the magnet, you transferred the magnet's magnetic properties to the needle. Once magnetized, the needle behaved the same way any other magnet would.

MAGNETIC SCREWDRIVER

What You'll Learn: You can use an electromagnet to magnetize a screwdriver.

What You'll Need: screwdriver; screws; electrical wire; 6-volt battery with screw-down terminals

Put a screwdriver next to several screws. If the screwdriver is not magnetized, nothing will happen. Coil a 3-foot piece of electrical wire around the metal shaft of the screwdriver about 20 times; make the loops close together, and leave about 10 inches of wire loose on each side of the coil. Connect the two loose ends of the wire to a 6-volt battery. The electric current flowing through the wire makes the screwdriver into a magnet. In a short time, the screwdriver will have become magnetized. Remove the screwdriver from the coil. Touch it to the screws. Do the screws cling to the screwdriver now?

178 PAPER CLIP CHAIN

What You'll Learn: Magnetism can be passed by induction.

What You'll Need: strong magnet; paper clips

Take a strong magnet, and hold a paper clip to it. Touch a second paper clip to the first one that is hanging from the magnet. The second paper clip will be attracted to the first one because the first clip has become a magnet. Continue adding paper clips in this way to see how long of a chain you can create. Take the first paper clip off the magnet. Do the other paper clips stay joined together, or do the other paper clips immediately fall?

HOT NEEDLES 179

What You'll Learn: A magnetized needle will quickly lose its magnetism if the needle is heated.

What You'll Need: needle; bar magnet; paper clip; candle; candleholder; matches; tongs

Caution: *This activity should be done with adult supervision.*

Magnetize a needle by stroking it in the same direction along a bar magnet about two dozen times. Hold the magnet away from the needle when you are moving it back to the eye of the needle. Test the needle with a paper clip to make sure it is magnetized. Put a candle securely in a candleholder, and light it. Using tongs, hold the needle in the flame of the candle for a few seconds. Take the needle out of the flame. Still holding the needle with the tongs, use the paper clip to test the needle to see if it's still magnetized. If the needle is still magnetic, put it back into the flame for a few more seconds, and test it again.

What Happened? The heat energy from the candle caused the molecules in the needle to move around in a way that disrupted the needle's magnetic field.

180 TIMELY MAGNETISM

What You'll Learn: You can magnetize a needle, but the magnetism will eventually leave the needle.

What You'll Need: needle; bar magnet; paper clip; paper and pen; watch or clock

Take a steel needle, and stroke it two dozen times, in the same direction each time, along a bar magnet. Each time, hold the needle away from the magnet as you move it in position to the top of the needle to stroke it again. Determine whether or not the needle is magnetized by seeing if it attracts a paper clip. If it is not magnetized, stroke it against the bar magnet until it is.

Once you've shown that your needle is magnetized, write down the time and date. Check the needle several times throughout the day to see if it is still magnetized. Each time, write down the time and whether or not the needle is still magnetized. Continue to check your needle a couple of times a day until it is no longer magnetized; remember to write down the time and results each time you check your magnet. How long did it take for the needle to lose its magnetism?

MIGHTY MAGNET 181

What You'll Learn: Some magnets are stronger than others.

What You'll Need: thread; two needles; two bar magnets; tape; two paper clips

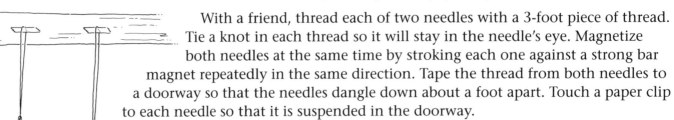

With a friend, thread each of two needles with a 3-foot piece of thread. Tie a knot in each thread so it will stay in the needle's eye. Magnetize both needles at the same time by stroking each one against a strong bar magnet repeatedly in the same direction. Tape the thread from both needles to a doorway so that the needles dangle down about a foot apart. Touch a paper clip to each needle so that it is suspended in the doorway.

Now wait to see which magnet lasts longer. How long does each needle remain magnetized? Which paper clip fell first, and which remained hanging from its magnet? How much longer did the remaining paper clip stay attached to its magnet?

Surface Tension

Surface tension is a property of liquids that causes the surface to behave something like an elastic skin. The molecules in the surface layer are strongly attracted by the molecules of liquid in the layer underneath, but they are not attracted by the molecules of air above them. This makes the molecules of the liquid stick together to some degree.

 ## ABSORB OR REPEL?

What You'll Learn: Some materials absorb and some materials repel water.

What You'll Need: paper and pen; various household items; water; eyedropper; magnifying glass

Label a sheet of paper "ABSORBS WATER." Label a second sheet of paper "REPELS WATER." Then find various objects around your house, such as pieces of cloth, a cotton ball, waxed paper, aluminum foil, newspaper, a magazine page, or a coffee filter. Predict whether the objects will absorb or repel water, and write your predictions down on the appropriate sheet of paper.

Set the objects on a table. Use an eyedropper to drop a few drops of water on each object. Use a magnifying glass to look closely at the water on each object to study how it interacts with the object's surface. Were you right or wrong on most of your predictions?

What Happened? The looseness or firmness of an object's surface is called its *porousness,* and it plays an important role in how water acts on the object's surface. The ability of a substance to attract or repel water molecules also plays a role. Things that soak up water are said to absorb water. If water beads up on a surface, that object is said to repel water.

183 WET NEEDLE

What You'll Learn: Water has surface tension that can support objects.
What You'll Need: bowl; water; needle; tissue paper; magnifying glass

Fill a bowl halfway with water. Drop a needle point-end first into the water, and watch as the needle sinks. Try setting the needle gently on the water lengthwise, and watch what happens. The needle will still sink.

Now take a piece of tissue paper about 3-inches square. Lay the needle on the piece of tissue paper, and gently set the tissue on the surface of the water in the bowl. The tissue with the needle on it will float and support the needle. When the tissue gets soaked with water, it will sink. But the needle will remain floating. Look at the needle through a magnifying glass. Can you see little dents around the needle in the water? It almost looks as if the surface of the water has a "skin."

What Happened? The molecules of water at the surface were attracted to each other by surface tension. The force of the surface tension was greater than the force of gravity on the needle, so the water held up the needle.

OVER THE TOP 184

What You'll Learn: You can stretch the surface of water.
What You'll Need: small plastic cup; water; eyedropper

Fill a small plastic cup all the way to the top with water. Hold an eyedropper filled with water close to the surface of the water in the plastic cup, and gently release the water drop by drop. How many drops can you add to the plastic cup after it is "full"? Can you see that the water level actually rises above the top of the cup? Water molecules attract one another strongly so that the water seems to hold together.

185 BREAK THE TENSION

What You'll Learn: The force of surface tension can be overcome.

What You'll Need: bowl; water; paper clip; fork; soap

Fill a small bowl halfway with water. Using a fork, gently lower a paper clip on top of the water. Pull the fork away carefully, and the paper clip will float. Look closely at the water around the paper clip. You may be able to see that the top of the water looks stretched. Very gently touch the top of the water with a bar of soap. The paper clip will sink.

What Happened? The soap interferes with the attraction that the water molecules have for each other. By disrupting the attraction, the soap breaks the surface tension that was supporting the paper clip.

CUTTING WATER 186

What You'll Learn: You can split a water drop into smaller drops, and you can put small water drops together.

What You'll Need: glass; water; food color; spoon; eyedropper; waxed paper; toothpick; drinking straw

Put a drop of food color into a glass of water; stir until all of the water is evenly colored. Using an eyedropper, gently put several drops of the colored water onto a sheet of waxed paper. Look at the circular shape of the drops.

With a toothpick, try to cut a water drop in half. Can you do it? With a drinking straw, blow gently to try to put two water drops together. Can you do it?

What Happened? The surface tension of water pulls the water molecules in a drop toward each other; the molecules in the outer layer are drawn in toward the center of the drop, giving the drop its round shape. The surface tension that holds the water in that shape affected how the water acted when you exerted force on it with the toothpick and the straw.

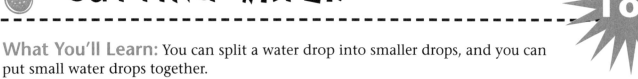

FLAT DROPS

187

What You'll Learn: The force of surface tension can be overcome.

What You'll Need: glass; water; straw; vinyl tablecloth; magnifying glass; flat toothpick; dish-washing liquid.

Fill a glass with water. Suck some of the water up in a straw, and quickly put your finger over the end of the straw to hold in the water. Gently release some water from the straw onto a vinyl tablecloth so that it forms several drops. Using a magnifying glass, look at the circular shape of the water drops. Now dip the end of a toothpick into some dish-washing liquid. Gently touch the tip of the toothpick to some of the water drops, and observe how the shape of the water drops changes.

What Happened? The surface tension of water pulls water molecules in a drop toward each other; the molecules in the outer layer are drawn in toward the center of the drop, giving the drop its round shape. The dish-washing liquid interfered with the attraction that the water molecules had for each other and changed the shape of the drops.

BUBBLES, BUBBLES EVERYWHERE

188

What You'll Learn: Bubbles get their shape from surface tension.

What You'll Need: dish-washing liquid; measuring cup and spoon; glycerin; water; large container; dish pan; pipe cleaners; plastic soda pop ring; scissors; stapler; wooden sticks

Add ½ cup of dish-washing liquid and 2 teaspoons of glycerin to ½ gallon of water in a large container. Mix the materials together, and let them sit overnight. The next day, pour the mixture into a plastic dish pan out in your back yard. Shape pipe cleaners into circles of different sizes. Cut a circle of plastic from a soda pop ring, and staple it to a wooden stick. Dip these devices into the bubble solution, and gently blow through the circles to make bubbles. Circles of different sizes will make bubbles of different sizes.

ENERGIZE ME

Anytime anything changes in the physical world, energy is involved. A moving car, a glowing lightbulb, and boiling water all depend on energy. Energy is the ability to do work or to make something change. Heat, electricity, and chemical energy are different forms of energy. Even though we use energy, we can never make or destroy any of it. We can only convert it from one form to another. In this chapter, you will explore types of energy around us and see how energy is converted from one form into another.

Forms of Energy

Scientists think of energy in two basic ways. *Potential* energy is energy that is stored, or not being used. *Kinetic* energy is energy that causes motion. Potential energy can change into kinetic energy, and kinetic energy can change into potential energy. For example, a ball held above the ground has potential energy. If the ball is dropped so that it falls to the ground, the potential energy is converted into kinetic energy.

IN THE SWING OF THINGS

189

What You'll Learn: In a pendulum, energy is repeatedly changed back and forth from kinetic energy to potential energy.

What You'll Need: a weight, such as a bolt, a key, or a rock; string; tape

Caution: *Be certain the swinging pendulum will not strike a person or a fragile object.*

Tie a weight to the end of a string. Tie the other end of the string to a railing or tape it to a table so that the string and weight can freely swing back and forth. Keeping the string taut, pull back the weight. While you are holding the weight, it has no kinetic energy because it is not moving. All of its energy is potential energy. Release the weight, and watch it swing. As it swings downward, the potential energy is converted into kinetic energy. When it reaches the bottom of its swing, all the energy is kinetic energy. As the weight starts rising up, the kinetic energy is converted into potential energy. When it reaches the high point of its swing, all of the kinetic energy is converted to potential energy. As the weight starts to fall downward, the process starts again. This conversion of potential energy to kinetic energy and back will continue as long as the pendulum swings.

THE TWIST

190

What You'll Learn: A rubber band can hold potential energy and convert it to kinetic energy.

What You'll Need: rubber band; padlock

Loop a rubber band around the U-shaped part of a padlock, and lock the padlock. Hold the end of the rubber band in one hand so the lock hangs from it, and turn the lock around five times with your other hand. As the rubber band twists, it stores some of the energy you used to turn the lock as potential energy. Now release the lock. The spinning lock has energy of motion, or kinetic energy. As it spins, it winds the rubber band in the other direction, and the rubber band again stores potential energy, which will be released when the lock spins the other way. Eventually the lock will stop twisting because it loses energy to friction.

191 THE COME-BACK CAN

What You'll Learn: You can use the principles of potential and kinetic energy to make a can that seems to change direction on its own.

What You'll Need: hammer; nail; empty coffee can with lid; rubber band; weight, such as a washer, nut, or bolt; two dowels

Use a hammer and nail to poke a hole in the center of the bottom of a coffee can. Use the nail to poke a hole in the center of the coffee can lid. Tie a weight, such as a washer, nut, or bolt, to the middle of a rubber band. Put the rubber band through the hole in the bottom of the can, so that one loop of the rubber band sticks outside the can and the rest of the rubber band (and the weight) is inside the can. Put a dowel through the loop to hold it in place on the outside of the can. Put the other end of the rubber band through the lid from the inside, so that a small loop of rubber band sticks out of the lid. Put the other dowel through this loop to hold it in place on top of the lid. Put the lid on the coffee can. Roll the can away from you on the floor. When it starts slowing down, yell, "Come back!" When the can stops rolling, it should reverse directions and roll back toward you. If it doesn't work, try using a different size of rubber band.

What Happened? The rolling can has kinetic energy, or energy of motion. As it rolls, the weight inside remains stationary, causing the rubber band to twist around; the rubber band gains potential energy from the kinetic energy of the can. When the can stops rolling, the rubber band unwinds and converts its potential energy into kinetic energy, sending the can back in the other direction.

192 SLINGSHOT SCIENCE

What You'll Learn: A slingshot converts potential energy into kinetic energy.

What You'll Need: hammer; nails; block of wood; thick rubber band; small plastic caps

Caution: *This project requires adult supervision. Never use your slingshot to shoot at anyone or anything.*

Hammer two nails about 3 inches apart into a piece of wood. Loop a thick rubber band from one nail to the other. Find a place where you can safely fling plastic caps without hitting anyone or anything. Place a plastic cap in the center of the rubber band, and pull back on the rubber band. Release the rubber band, and watch as the rubber band flings the cap. The energy you used to pull the rubber band back was stored as potential energy while you held the rubber band in place. When you released it, the potential energy was converted into the kinetic energy of the moving plastic cap.

Experiment with your slingshot. Which goes farther, a light cap or a heavy cap? What other properties of caps influence their flight? Does the distance you pull the rubber band affect how far the caps fly? Try it with larger and smaller rubber bands, and observe the differences.

TENNIS CANNON 193

What You'll Learn: The kinetic energy in one object can be transferred to another object.

What You'll Need: basketball; tennis ball

Hold a basketball in one hand and a tennis ball in the other, and drop them to the ground from the same height. Watch carefully to see how high they bounce. Did one bounce higher than the other? Now hold the basketball in one hand, and place the tennis ball on top of the basketball with your other hand. Drop them to the ground together. Watch carefully to see how high they bounce.

What Happened? The tennis ball and basketball have energy from falling. The amount of energy depends on the weight of the object. The basketball is much heavier, so it contains much more energy. When the tennis ball and basketball hit the ground, all of the energy of the falling basketball is transferred to the tennis ball, and it launches the tennis ball like a cannon.

194 WHEEL FUN

What You'll Learn: Raised water has potential energy and releases it as kinetic energy when it falls.

What You'll Need: two thin wires; cork; 14 paper clips; running water

Place one thin wire in each end of a cork. Unbend the first curve in each of the paper clips. Insert the ends of 12 paper clips into the middle of the cork at even intervals around its diameter. Arrange the paper clips so all of the loops are in line with each other. You now have a water wheel. Pick up the water wheel with the two remaining paper clips by slipping the loop of one paper clip over the wire in each end of the cork. Turn on a faucet, and hold the water wheel under the running water so that the water strikes the paper clips.

What Happened? The water in the faucet has potential energy. When it falls, that energy is converted to kinetic energy. Your water wheel captured some of that energy and used it to spin around. Large water wheels have been used for centuries to grind wheat and corn. Today, water turbines use the same principle to generate electricity.

WATER WHEEL CHALLENGE 195

What You'll Learn: You can design your own water wheel to convert the potential energy of water into kinetic energy.

This is the Water Wheel Challenge! After reading and doing the activity Wheel Fun, you are ready for this challenge. Design and construct your own water wheel that will spin when placed under water. Build several water wheels, using different materials or altering your design slightly to see which one works best.

CAR TALK

196

What You'll Learn: Moving cars get their kinetic energy from the stored chemical energy in gasoline; this is sometimes called chemical potential energy. The design of the car influences how far it can go with the same amount of energy.

A moving car has kinetic energy—the energy of motion. This energy comes from the stored energy in gasoline. Have an adult take you to a new car dealership. Each car has a sticker in the window that tells the number of miles the car can go with one gallon of gas; this is called gas mileage. Each car has a different number for driving on highways and for driving in cities. Compare cars that can go a long distance on one gallon of gasoline with cars that can go shorter distances. What differences can you see between the cars? Talk with the adult who brought you about why certain cars have higher or lower mileage numbers.

Energy Conductors

Conductors allow energy to flow through them easily. Insulators make it difficult for energy to flow through them. We use insulators to keep food hot and to make electrical wires safe to handle. We use conductors to transfer energy from one place to another.

I'M MELTING

What You'll Learn: Different materials conduct heat at different rates.

What You'll Need: different flat materials, such as a ceramic plate, plastic plate, steel pot, copper pot, or wooden bowl; ice cubes; pen and paper

Gather several flat surfaces made from different materials, such as a ceramic plate, plastic plate, steel pot, or wooden bowl. Take several ice cubes that are about the same size, and put one on each surface. Let them sit undisturbed, and watch as the ice melts. Write down the surfaces in the order that their ice cubes melted.

What Happened? Ice needs heat to melt. Some heat will come from the surface it is on. Ice will melt faster on a surface that is a good conductor of heat and slower on a surface that is not a good conductor.

HEAT SHEET

What You'll Learn: Different materials conduct heat at different rates.

What You'll Need: paper; scissors; aluminum foil; two thermometers; pen and paper

Cut a strip of paper about 8 inches long and 2 inches wide. Cut a strip of aluminum foil the same size. Wrap about 1 inch of the paper around the bulb of a thermometer. Wrap about 1 inch of the aluminum foil around the bulb of another thermometer. Find a windowsill that has an area in the shade and an area in the sun. Put the two thermometers on the windowsill so that the thermometers are completely in the shade but the ends of the paper and aluminum foil are in the sun. Record the starting temperatures for both thermometers. Then record the temperatures every few minutes.

What Happened? The thermometer with the foil heated to a higher temperature because the aluminum is a better conductor of heat. Energy from the sunlight heated the aluminum foil and paper. Aluminum is a good conductor of heat, so it transferred much of the heat to the thermometer. Paper is a poor conductor of heat, so it transferred little of the heat to the thermometer.

PROBING FOR CONDUCTORS

199

What You'll Learn: Some materials allow electricity to flow through them and some do not.

What You'll Need: electrical wire; D battery; tape; 1.5-volt lightbulb and holder; various household objects, such as pencil, paper clip, fabric, key, spoon, etc.

Caution: *Wires can become hot during this activity.*

Tape the end of a piece of electrical wire to the top of a D battery. Tape the end of a second wire to the bottom of the battery. If you attach these to a lightbulb stand, it should make the lightbulb light. (If you have a lightbulb with no stand, hold one wire at the bottom of the bulb, and hold the other wire on the side to light the bulb.)

Disconnect the first wire from the lightbulb, and connect a third wire to the bulb in its place. Wire 1 will have one end connected to the battery and the other end free. Wire 2 will have one end connected to the battery and the other end connected to the bulb. Wire 3 will have one end connected to the bulb and the other end free.

Touch the end of wire 1 to the end of wire 3; the lightbulb should light. These two wires are the probes. Touch the ends of the probes to a pencil, making sure the probes don't touch each other. If the pencil is an electrical conductor, the electricity from the battery will flow through it and light the bulb. If the pencil is an electrical insulator, the electricity will not flow through it, and the bulb will not light. Test the other objects you gathered to see if they are insulators or conductors.

200 HOT MUGS

What You'll Learn: Insulators don't conduct heat well, and they can be used to keep things warm or to keep things cool.

What You'll Need: mugs made of different materials, such as ceramic, glass, or plastic; hot water; measuring cup; thermometer; paper and pen; clock

Gather a variety of mugs made from different materials, such as ceramic, glass, or plastic. It is best if the mugs are all about the same size. Using a measuring cup, carefully fill each mug with the same amount of hot water. Take the temperature of each mug every 3 minutes with a thermometer. Make a chart to record all the temperatures. Take a total of seven readings on each mug. Look at your data to determine which material makes the best insulator.

Friction

When surfaces rub against each other, they create friction. The molecules from the two surfaces catch on each other as they pass back and forth.

Getting the molecules to move past each other uses up energy, so friction slows things down. It also makes the molecules vibrate, which generates heat.

HOT HANDS

What You'll Learn: Friction produces heat.

Rub your two hands together. Do this quickly, and feel the heat produced. When your hands rub against each other, they produce friction. This friction produces heat.

GIVE ME A BREAK

What You'll Learn: Friction uses up the energy of a moving object.
What You'll Need: bicycle with hand brakes

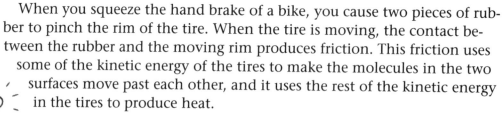

When you squeeze the hand brake of a bike, you cause two pieces of rubber to pinch the rim of the tire. When the tire is moving, the contact between the rubber and the moving rim produces friction. This friction uses some of the kinetic energy of the tires to make the molecules in the two surfaces move past each other, and it uses the rest of the kinetic energy in the tires to produce heat.

Before you get on your bike, feel the rubber of the rear brake pads to roughly determine their temperature. Get on your bicycle, and pedal to build speed. Now put the rear brakes on so the bicycle comes to a slow stop. Get off your bike, and feel the rear brake pads. They will be warm, or even hot, from the heat produced by the friction. Disc brakes on a car stop the car using the same principle.

203 ROUGH STUFF

What You'll Learn: Sandpaper rubbed on wood produces friction and heat.

What You'll Need: wood; sandpaper

Feel a piece of wood to roughly determine its temperature. Now rub it with some sandpaper. Do this vigorously for about a minute. Now feel the wood. It is very warm. Sandpaper creates a great deal of friction when it is rubbed on wood. In addition to sanding the wood to make it smoother, the friction creates heat.

SHAKEN, NOT STIRRED 204

What You'll Learn: Friction produces heat.

What You'll Need: coffee can with lid; sand; thermometer; pen and paper

Fill a coffee can halfway with sand. Measure the temperature of the sand, and write it down. Remove the thermometer, place the lid securely on the can, and shake the can rapidly for a few minutes. Measure the temperature of the sand, and write it down again. Repeat the test one more time.

What Happened? The energy you used to shake up the can made the sand particles rub against each other and against the side of the can. This created friction, and the friction produced heat. The sand particles acted in a similar way to molecules from two different surfaces that are rubbed against each other.

BALLOON HOVERCRAFT

205

What You'll Learn: Air can be used as a lubricant to reduce friction between objects.

What You'll Need: plastic soda bottle; knife; nail or other sturdy pointed object; balloon

Caution: *This project requires adult supervision.*

Carefully cut off the top of a large plastic soda bottle about 2 inches from the top of the bottle. Cut evenly so the bottle top will sit flat. Poke a small hole in the bottle cap with a nail. Screw the cap back on the bottle top, and set the bottle top on a flat surface. Gently shove the bottle top to see how far it will slide over the table top. Blow up a balloon. Pinch the neck of the balloon to keep the air from escaping, and stretch the opening of the balloon securely over the bottle cap. Let go of the balloon, and watch as the bottle top rises above the table. Gently shove the bottle top, and it will glide easily over the surface of the table.

What Happened? As the air escaped from the balloon through the opening in the cap, it pushed down against the table and lifted the bottle top. The bottle was no longer touching the table, so there was less friction for the bottle top to overcome and it could move farther.

 # HOT WIRED

206

What You'll Learn: Friction can be produced by moving a single substance.

Take a piece of thick wire, such as a coat hanger, and feel it to roughly determine its temperature. Bend the wire back and forth in the same spot eight or ten times. (Don't bend it too many times, or it may break and have sharp points on the ends.) Now feel the spot where you were bending. The wire has become warm in this area.

What Happened? The bending caused friction between the molecules in that area of the wire. The friction produced heat energy, which you felt when you touched the wire.

Static Electricity

Static electricity occurs when a charge builds up in an object. Objects become charged by either losing or gaining electrons. Electrons have a negative charge, so an object becomes negatively charged if it gains electrons. If an object loses electrons, it becomes positively charged. Remember one thing about this section. Static electricity activities don't work well if it's too humid. If the activities don't work, try them on a drier day.

207 YOU REPULSE ME

What You'll Learn: A charged object will repel another object with the same type of charge.

What You'll Need: two balloons; string; tape; cloth (wool, polyester, or nylon)

Blow up two balloons. Tie each to a string about 15 inches long. Tape the strings to the edge of a table so the balloons hang down about 1 inch apart from each other. Charge one balloon by rubbing it with a cloth. Then charge the other balloon in the same way. Let both balloons hang near each other, and watch what they do.

What Happened? Rubbing balloons with the cloth transferred electrons to the balloons. This made both balloons negatively charged. When the balloons were brought near each other, the charge acted to push the balloons away from each other. Objects with the same charge repel each other.

YOU SHOCK ME

208

What You'll Learn: When you charge an object, it will lose its charge through another conductor.

You have probably gotten shocks from static electricity many times. Rub your feet on carpet as you walk in a room. Touch a metal doorknob. Do this again, and touch a friend. As you rubbed your feet along the carpet, your body picked up an electrical charge. When you touched something that conducted electricity, such as a metal object or another person, the charge passed from you to the other conductor. One or both of you felt a shock, and you may have even seen a spark.

STICKY BALLOONS

209

What You'll Learn: A charged object can stick to a neutral object by inducing an opposite charge.

What You'll Need: balloon; cloth (wool, polyester, or nylon)

Rub a cloth on a balloon, or rub a balloon on your hair. Put the balloon up against a wall, and let go. Time how long it stays on the wall. Try different cloths and different wall surfaces to see which makes the balloon stick the longest. Make sure you rub it the same number of times each time you charge it to make the comparisons fair.

What Happened? The balloon rubbed with the cloth became negatively charged. When brought near the wall, the negatively charged balloon repelled electrons in the surface of the wall, and created a positive charge on the surface of the wall. Opposite charges attract, so the negative balloon stuck to the positive wall surface. But as the balloon lost charge to the air and wall, the attraction decreased, and eventually the balloon fell.

210 TRICKLE DOWN ACTIVITY

What You'll Learn: A charged object can curve the path of water trickling from a faucet.

What You'll Need: balloon or comb; cloth (wool, polyester, or nylon); faucet

Charge a comb or balloon by rubbing it with a cloth. Turn a faucet on so the water falls in a slow, gentle stream. Place the balloon or comb near the falling water, and watch how the water acts.

What Happened? By rubbing the balloon or comb, you caused it to have a charge of static electricity. The negative charge of the object acted to repel the negative charge that the moving water had, causing the water to change its path.

ELECTRO-DETECTO

211

What You'll Learn: You can make a device that detects electrical charges.

What You'll Need: bottle; cork; nail; electrical wire; thin foil

Find a bottle and a cork that will seal it. With a nail, make a small hole through the center of the cork from top to bottom. Push a 6-inch piece of heavy electrical wire through the hole. Leave about 1 inch of wire above the top of the cork.

Bend the wire coming from the bottom of the cork into a flat hook, shaped like the bottom of a coat hanger. Cut a piece of aluminum foil into a strip 1 inch long and ¼ inch wide. Fold the strip in half, and hang it on the flat hook. Put the hook and foil into the bottle, and seal the opening with the cork. Make sure the foil and the hook do not touch the sides or bottom of the jar. Roll up another piece of aluminum foil into a tight ball about 1 inch in diameter around the wire sticking out of the cork. Make sure that the ball is smooth and tightly packed.

You have just built a functional electroscope that will tell you if any object carries a charge. If you hold an object with a charge near the foil ball, the object will draw the opposite charge through the wire from the foil strip. The two sides of the strip will then have the same charge and repel each other.

212 DETECTING CHARGED OBJECTS

What You'll Learn: An electroscope can detect the amount of charge an object contains.

What You'll Need: balloon or comb; cloth (wool, polyester, or nylon); electroscope (see Electro-Detecto on page 141)

Turn a balloon or comb into a charged object by rubbing it with a cloth. Bring the charged object near (but don't touch) the foil ball at the top of the electroscope. Watch the foil leaves swing apart. Rub the balloon or comb with the cloth again for a longer time to increase the charge. Hold the charged object near the foil ball of the electroscope again, and observe the leaves of the foil strip. Do they move even farther this time? The increased charge of the charged object made the leaves have an even stronger charge, so they repelled each other with greater force.

CHARGING BY CONDUCTION 213

Turn a balloon or plastic comb into a charged object by rubbing it with a cloth. Then rub the charged object on the top of an electroscope (see Electro-Detecto on page 141). Repeat this several times until the electroscope's foil leaves swing apart. Placing a charge on the electroscope by touching it with a charged object is called charging by conduction. As you add more charge, the leaves swing farther apart. The leaves of the electroscope stay apart as long as they have a charge. Touch the top of the electroscope with your finger. Instantly, the leaves of the electroscope fall together.

What Happened? When you rub the charged object on the electroscope, the negative charge on the object is transferred to the ball of the electroscope. These negative charges are conducted to the leaves of the electroscope. When the charge build up is sufficient, the leaves will push away from each other. The more charge you add, the more they push away. When you touch the electroscope with your finger, you give a path for the electrons to leave the electroscope. When the leaves of the electroscope lose their charge, they will stop repelling each other.

214 CHARGING BY INDUCTION

Turn a balloon or plastic comb into a charged object by rubbing it with a cloth. Bring the charged object near (but not touching) the ball of an electroscope (see Electro-Detecto on page 141). When the foil leaves push apart, keep the balloon or comb near, and touch the ball of the electroscope with your finger. The leaves collapse. Remove your finger, and remove the balloon or comb. Notice the leaves now repel each other. They have been charged by induction. Now bring a charged balloon or comb near the electroscope. The leaves repel each other with less force; they move closer together.

What Happened? Holding the negatively charged object near the top of the electroscope pushed electrons from the top of the electroscope, and some went to the bottom. When you touched the top, some of the electrons left the electroscope and entered your body. When you removed your finger and the charged object, the electroscope became positively charged. Bringing a negatively charged object near the top of the electroscope then caused the leaves to fall. This is because electrons are pushed into the leaves, reducing the positive charge. If you touch the electroscope with a wire or your finger, it will lose its charge.

 # SNAKE CHARMER 215

What You'll Learn: A charged object can stick to a neutral object by inducing an opposite charge.

What You'll Need: string; tape; balloon; cloth (wool, polyester, or nylon)

Tape one end of a 5-inch piece of string to a table top. Charge a balloon by rubbing it with a cloth. Bring the balloon near the untaped end of string to make the string rise off the table. Move the balloon back and forth to make the string sway.

What Happened? The balloon rubbed with the cloth became negatively charged. When brought near the string, it repelled the electrons at the surface of the string. The surface of the string became positively charged and was attracted to the balloon. You can see that the energy of static electricity can be used to do work, such as lifting up the string. Do you think you could charge the balloon enough so that it would lift up the table? Why not?

STATIC CLING JACKS

216

What You'll Learn: A charged object can stick to a neutral object by inducing an opposite charge.

What You'll Need: paper; plastic comb; cloth (wool, polyester, or nylon)

Tear up a sheet of thin paper into small pieces. Rub a comb with a cloth to give it a charge. Hold the comb near the pieces of paper, and watch as they cling to the comb. Play a version of the game jacks called Static Cling Jacks with a friend or by yourself. Put the pieces of paper in a pile. Rub the comb a little so that it only picks up one piece of paper. Rub the comb a little more so it picks up exactly two pieces of paper. Then try for three. Keep going until you pick up more or less than the correct number. At this point, you lose your turn and the next player goes. When it is your turn, you start with one piece of paper again. Can you work your way up to picking up eight pieces of paper?

Current Electricity

Current electricity is the flow of electrons. To make a current of electricity, the electrons need to flow in a complete, unbroken circle. The path for electricity is called a *circuit.*
If the circuit is not complete, the electrons will not be able to flow.
Moving electrons contain energy, and this energy can be used in many ways.
Remember that electricity is a powerful force, and it can be dangerous. The projects in this section use small amounts of electricity generated by batteries.
Never experiment with the electricity that flows through the outlets in your house; it is much more powerful and can cause serious injury.

POWER METERS

217

With an adult, find the electrical power meter for your home. It contains four dials in a row. Read the number each dial is pointing to, and write them all down in order from left to right; if the pointer is between two numbers, choose the lower number. This gives you a four-digit number of kilowatt hours of electricity. Read your home's meter at the start of the week. Then read it at the end of the week. Subtract the first number from the second number. The difference is the amount of electricity used in your home between the two meter readings.

Think of ways to save electricity, such as turning off lights and appliances when you're not using them. Use these approaches during the next week, and then check the meter again to see if you and your family used less electricity the second week than you did the first week.

LIGHT ON

218

What You'll Learn: You can make a complete electrical circuit.

What You'll Need: 1.5-volt flashlight bulb; electrical wire; D battery

Caution: *Wires can become hot during this activity.*

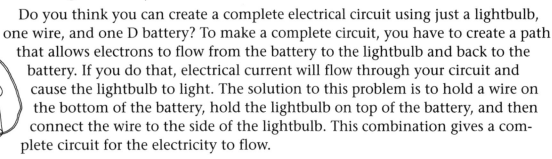

Do you think you can create a complete electrical circuit using just a lightbulb, one wire, and one D battery? To make a complete circuit, you have to create a path that allows electrons to flow from the battery to the lightbulb and back to the battery. If you do that, electrical current will flow through your circuit and cause the lightbulb to light. The solution to this problem is to hold a wire on the bottom of the battery, hold the lightbulb on top of the battery, and then connect the wire to the side of the lightbulb. This combination gives a complete circuit for the electricity to flow.

219 LIGHT ON BRIGHTER

What You'll Learn: You can make a complete circuit with two batteries.

What You'll Need: 1.5-volt flashlight bulb; electrical wire; two D batteries

Caution: *Wires can become hot during this activity.*

This is a new challenge. Do you think you can create a complete electrical circuit using just a lightbulb, one wire, and *two* D batteries? Remember, you still have to make a complete path for the electrons to flow from the batteries to the lightbulb and back to the batteries. The solution to this problem is to stack the batteries on top of each other, with the bottom of one battery on the top of the other. Then hold a wire to the bottom of the bottom battery, hold the lightbulb on top of the top battery, and connect the wire to the side of the lightbulb. How does the brightness of this bulb compare to when only one battery is used?

BATTERY TESTER 220

What You'll Learn: A battery tester can be made with wire and a flashlight bulb. The brightness of the bulb is an indicator of the strength of the battery.

What You'll Need: electrical wire; pliers; 1.5-volt lightbulb; batteries

Caution: *Wires can become hot during this activity. Do not test large batteries such as those used for cars.*

Twist a small loop in the center of a 5-inch piece of stiff electrical wire; this loop will be used as a handle for your tester. If you are using very thick wire, you can use pliers to help twist the loop. Wrap the top end of the wire around the metal bottom of a 1.5-volt lightbulb. Curl the other end up and around so it points toward the bottom of the lightbulb. Leave a little less space between the wire end and the bulb than a battery would occupy.

To use your battery tester, slide a battery into the tester so the top of the battery makes contact with the bottom of the bulb and the bottom of the battery makes contact with the free end of the wire. Use a new battery to make sure your tester is working. If it doesn't work, check the connections. When it does work, start testing the D batteries around your home. If batteries do not light the bulb, they have lost their power. Some batteries may be weak and will only dimly light the bulb. See if you can design a battery tester for rectangular 9-volt batteries.

SWITCH IT

221

What You'll Learn: A switch can be used to open and close a circuit.

What You'll Need: 1.5-volt lightbulb; socket for bulb; electrical wire; D battery; tape; aluminum foil; scissors

Caution: *Wires can become hot during this activity.*

Screw a 1.5-volt lightbulb into a socket, and connect a wire to each of the screws of the socket. Tape one wire to the bottom of a D battery. Tape the other wire to the top of the battery. The bulb should light. Remove the wire from the bottom of the battery.

Now make a switch. Cut a strip of aluminum foil about 2 inches long and 1 inch wide. Fold it in half lengthwise, and then fold it over about one third of the way from the end. Tape the shorter end of the strip to the table top. Cut another strip of aluminum foil about 1 inch long and 1 inch wide, and fold it in half lengthwise. Tape this strip to the table top so that when the longer strip is held flat on the table, they make contact with each other. Take the wire that had been on the bottom of the battery, and slide the free end under one of the pieces of aluminum foil; tape it in place. Slide the end of a third wire under the other piece of aluminum foil, tape it in place, and tape the other end to the bottom of the battery. You have just made a complete circuit with a switch.

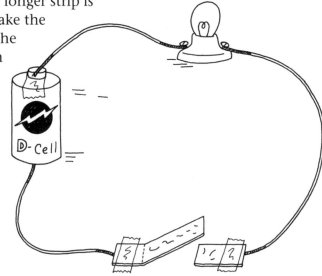

Push down the folded piece of aluminum foil so it touches the other piece of aluminum foil. The bulb will light up. When the foil pieces are touching, the electrons have a complete path to flow from the battery to the bulb and back. When the foil pieces are not touching, the electrons do not have a complete path, and the bulb will not light up.

LIGHT IS RIGHT!

222

What You'll Learn: You can use complete circuits to make a quiz board.

What You'll Need: cardboard; brads; marker; electrical wire; 1.5-volt lightbulb; 9-volt battery; tape

Caution: *Wires can become hot during this activity.*

In this project, you create a quiz card. Think of pairs of items that can be matched. They can be states and their capitals, sports teams and their cities, chemical names and their formulas, or anything you can think of. Push six brads into a piece of cardboard in two vertical rows of three each. If you chose states and capitals, make the left row represent the states and the right row represent the capitals. Write the names of the states and capitals on the cardboard next to the brads.

On the back of the cardboard, connect an electrical wire to each brad that represents a state; connect the other end of each wire to the brad that represents that state's capital. Tape a 1.5-volt lightbulb to the back of

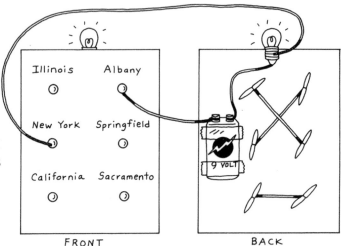

the card so it sticks above the top of the cardboard, and tape a 9-volt battery to the cardboard just below the bulb. Connect a wire from one terminal of the battery to the bottom of the bulb, and tape it in place. Connect another wire to the side of the base of the bulb. This wire should be long enough so that the other end can reach the front of the cardboard and touch any of the brads on the left; it will be one probe. Connect a wire to the other terminal of the battery. This wire should be long enough so that the other end can reach the front of the cardboard and touch any of the brads on the right; it will be the other probe. Cover the back of the quiz board with another sheet of cardboard.

Now touch the probe for the left side to any of the brads on the left. Choose the matching answer, and touch that brad with the other probe. The light should light. Positive reinforcement for a correct answer!

Design your own more complex quiz cards. Have more than three questions. Have some answers match with more than one correct item. For a real challenge, try to make one that has a buzzer that goes off if you select the wrong answer, as well as a light that goes on for the correct answer.

Magnetism

When electrons flow through a wire, they create magnetic fields. The discovery that moving electrons create magnetic fields was the first step in developing electric motors. It also led to the creation of the generator, which we use today for various reasons, such as producing electrical power for homes and industry.

223 COMPASS TURBULENCE

What You'll Learn: Electricity flowing through a wire creates a magnetic field.

What You'll Need: compass; electrical wire; D battery

Caution: *Wires can become hot during this activity.*

Hold a compass next to a piece of electrical wire. Note that the compass points to the north. Connect one end of the wire to the top of a D battery and the other to the bottom. Hold the compass near the wire now. Does the compass still point to the north? Move the compass to different locations around the wire to see how it is affected. How far away from the wire can the compass be and still be affected?

What Happened? The electricity flowing through the wire created a magnetic field around the wire. The magnetic field attracted the needle of the compass and caused it to change directions.

COILED MAGNETISM

224

What You'll Learn: A coiled wire produces a stronger magnetic field than an uncoiled wire.

What You'll Need: electrical wire; cardboard toilet paper tube; D battery; compass

Caution: *Wires can become hot during this activity.*

Coil electrical wire around a cardboard toilet paper tube so that it looks like a spring. This is called a *solenoid*. Connect one end of the wire to the top of a D battery. Connect the other end to the bottom of the battery. Move a compass to different locations around the solenoid, and note which direction the compass needle points. On one end of the solenoid, the compass needle points toward the center of the tube. On the other end, it points away from the center of the tube. Take another piece of wire, and attach one end to the top of the battery and the other end to the bottom of the battery. Compare the strength of the solenoid with the strength of a single stretched-out wire. The solenoid produces a bigger magnetic field.

ELECTROMAGNETIC MOMENTS

225

What You'll Learn: A solenoid can be made more powerful by putting a metal object in its center.

What You'll Need: electrical wire; D battery; paper clips; iron nail

Caution: *Wires can become hot during this activity.*

Coil a length of electrical wire so that it looks like a spring. This is called a *solenoid*. Connect one end of the wire to the top of a battery, and connect the other end to the bottom of the battery. The current flowing through the solenoid creates a magnetic field. See how many paper clips you can pick up with the solenoid. It might not work well because the magnetic field is not concentrated. Now wrap the same wire around an iron nail; make the same number of coils in the wire as you did the first time. Connect the wire to the battery. Now see how many paper clips the solenoid can pick up.

What Happened? The nail concentrated the magnetic field and allowed more nails to be picked up.

Energy from the Sun

The sun is an enormous nuclear furnace. Every second, tons of matter in the sun are converted to energy through nuclear fusion. Much of this energy is projected out into space as light and heat, and some of it reaches the Earth in the form of sunlight. The energy in sunlight is the source of most of the energy available to us on Earth, regardless of what form the energy takes.

226 SUN POWER

Think about the different sources of energy you see or use every day. Electrical energy in your home is generated by power plants that may use water, wind, or coal to generate electricity. Your car uses gasoline, which is a fossil fuel that contains chemical energy. Your body takes the chemical energy from the foods you eat and uses it throughout the day in many ways.

Do some research into each of these types of energy. Find out where it comes from. Where does the energy in the food you eat come from? What are fossil fuels made from, and where do they get the chemical energy they contain? How do power plants use moving wind and water to make electricity, and where does the energy that makes the wind and water move come from? You may be surprised to learn that the sun is involved in every one of these processes.

WARM PLANET, COLD PLANET

227

What You'll Learn: A covering that allows light to enter but slows the loss of heat causes an object to become warm.

What You'll Need: two thermometers; two identical jars; clear plastic wrap; paper and pen

Put a thermometer into each of two identical jars. Cover one jar with plastic wrap, and leave the other one uncovered. Record the temperatures in both jars. Place both jars next to each other on a sunny windowsill for about 20 minutes. Check and record the temperatures of the jars every few minutes. Compare how quickly the temperatures of the two jars rise. Take the jars off the windowsill, and put them somewhere out of the sun for about 20 minutes. Read and record the temperatures of the jars again every few minutes. Compare how quickly the temperatures of the two jars fall.

What Happened? The jar with the plastic wrap warmed faster and to a higher temperature than the jar without the plastic wrap. The plastic wrap let in the light, and it helped keep the heat inside. The other jar had no covering to hold in the heat. When you took the jars out of the sun, the one with the plastic wrap stayed warmer longer, again because the plastic wrap helped to keep in some of the heat. The gases in the Earth's atmosphere act in a similar way. They let sunlight in and help the Earth keep some of the heat. A planet without an atmosphere is usually cold because it loses heat quickly, just like the jar without the plastic wrap.

SUN PATCHES

228

What You'll Learn: Plants use the sun to make food.

What You'll Need: geranium plant; aluminum foil; tape; water; pot; stove; tongs; alcohol; coffee mug; spoon; iodine; measuring cup; eyedropper

Caution: *This project requires adult supervision.*

Put a geranium plant in a dark area for three days. Then cover a couple of leaves with aluminum foil (tape the foil in place if necessary), and leave the other leaves uncovered. Put the plant in the sun for three days.

On the fourth day, remove two leaves that were not covered with foil. Heat a pot of water until it boils, and place the leaves in the pot for 2 minutes. Turn off the heat, and remove the pot from the stove. Remove the leaves from the pot with tongs.

Pour about 1 inch of rubbing alcohol into a large coffee mug. Put the mug into the pot of hot water. (NOTE: Alcohol should not be directly heated on the stove because it can burn.)

Place the leaves into the alcohol in the mug. The warm alcohol helps to remove the green chloro-phyll from the leaves. Stir the solution to help the process. Remove the white leaves, and allow them to dry. Put about 10 drops of iodine into ½ cup of water to make an iodine solution. Place a drop of iodine solution on the leaves. The iodine should turn a blue-black color, indicating there is starch in the leaves.

Repeat this process with leaves that were covered with aluminum foil and did not get light. When the iodine is put on these leaves, it will not change color because there is no starch in the leaves.

What Happened? The plant's leaves use the sun's energy to create sugars, which the plant then converts into starch. When the leaves do not receive sunlight, there is no energy available to them to make food.

IT'S A WILD LIFE

The world around us is filled with all kinds of living things—fish, birds, insects, trees, mushrooms, people, worms, and many, many other life-forms. You probably think of these organisms as being very different from each other, but in many ways they are the same. They all need food, air, and water to survive. They all depend on other creatures, and they must be able to fit into their surroundings to survive. In this chapter, you will learn about the things that all life-forms do for survival.

Adaptation

Living things must be adaptable in order to survive. Conditions in the environment can change over days and over centuries, and organisms must find ways to cope with those changes. From cold polar regions to sweltering tropics, from high mountain peaks to the bottom of the sea, living things have adapted to conditions all over the Earth.

229 DOWN AND DIRTY

What You'll Learn: Soil contains microscopic animals that breathe.

What You'll Need: garden soil; jar with a lid; small container; limewater, which is available at a drugstore

Drop a large handful of garden soil into the bottom of a big empty jar. Pour some limewater into a small container. Note what the limewater looks like. Set the container of limewater, uncovered, inside the large jar so it rests on top of the soil. Tightly screw on the lid of the large jar, and leave it undisturbed. In two or three days, look at the limewater to see if it has changed in any way.

What Happened? The soil contains many microscopic animals. These animals take in oxygen and release carbon dioxide as a waste product, just as you do when you breathe. The limewater turned a milky color because the carbon dioxide produced by the organisms in the soil combined with the limewater to produce chalk. Your garden soil may contain bacteria, protozoans, and threadlike worms called nematodes.

 # WORM RACES 230

What You'll Learn: Worms prefer damp places.

What You'll Need: books; paper; water; worms

Put two books on a table, leaving a 1-inch gap between them. Lay a piece of paper over each book. Sprinkle water on one of the pieces of paper. Place a worm on the dry paper, and watch as it crosses the gap between the books to get to the moist paper. Put several worms onto the dry paper. Watch to see which one crosses over to the other side first.

LIFE ON A BRICK

What You'll Learn: You can grow grass on a brick.

What You'll Need: nonglazed porous brick; bowl; water; pie tin; grass seed

Many plants can adapt to very difficult growing conditions. Grass seeds, for example, can sprout in less than ideal locations. Soak a nonglazed brick overnight in a bowl of water. The next day, put the brick in a pie tin. Set the pie tin in a sunny spot. Pour water over the brick so that it runs down into the tin until the brick is sitting in about ½ inch of water. Sprinkle grass seed on the top of the brick. The grass seeds will sprout into plants.

PLANTS FROM LEAVES

What You'll Learn: Plants can be grown from leaves.

What You'll Need: African violet plant; scissors; clear plastic cup; water; paper and pen; four flowerpots; string; small rocks; vermiculite; potting soil; four saucers

Using scissors, snip off four healthy leaves from an African violet plant. Set these leaves in a clear plastic cup of water in a sunny window. Write down the date when you began this activity. Check on the leaves once a day. If you notice any change, write down your observations and the date. Eventually small leaves and new roots will begin to grow from the leaves.

Prepare four flowerpots for your sprouting leaves. Put a string through the hole in the bottom of each pot. Put an inch of small rocks for drainage in the bottom of each pot. Fill the pots with a mixture of potting soil and vermiculite. Plant each of the sprouting leaves in its own pot. Put each pot on a saucer, being sure that the string you put in the soil dangles down through the hole of the pot onto the saucer. Pour water into each saucer. The string will allow water from the saucer to travel up into the pot to keep the soil moist. Water as needed, and watch as a whole plant grows from each of the leaves you picked.

GULPING FISH

What You'll Learn: Water temperature affects a fish's ability to take in oxygen.

What You'll Need: two aquariums; four comet goldfish; two aquarium thermometers; paper and pen

Fish don't breathe the way you do, but they do get oxygen by gulping in water and pumping it over their gills. The gills are able to take oxygen from the water.

Set up two small fish tanks to hold two comet goldfish each. (Get advice from your local aquarium store on setting up the tanks.) Once the fish are settled into their new home, observe the temperature of the water by checking the tank thermometer. It should be close to room temperature, between 65° and 70°F. Watch each of the four fish, and determine how many times per minute they gulp to take air from the water. Write these figures down.

Gradually add warm water to one tank until, over a period of 20 minutes, you raise the temperature 5°F. Gradually add cool water to the other tank until, over a period of 20 minutes, you lower the temperature 5°F. Do not change the temperature too fast, as this can be harmful to the fish. Record the gulping rates of all four fish again.

What Happened? The fish gulped faster in warm water than in cool water. Warm water contains less oxygen than cool water, so fish in warm water have to work harder to get the oxygen they need from the water.

STRONG AND PUNY

234

Take six plants of the same variety, and plant them in pots with the same mixture of soil. Put them side by side in a warm sunny spot where they'll be exposed to the same temperatures and amount of sunlight. Give each of the plants the same amount of water, but water two of them with ordinary tap water, water two with vinegar water (1 tablespoonful of vinegar to 1 pint of water), and water two with water that contains added plant fertilizer. Observe the plants over several weeks, and make notes to describe their growth. Can you see differences between those that received vinegar water, those that received tap water, and those that received fertilizer?

BEANS IN THE DARK

235

What You'll Learn: Beans grown in the dark will behave differently from those grown in the light.

What You'll Need: lima beans; glass; water; two plastic foam cups; small rocks; sand; potting soil

Soak six lima beans overnight in a glass of water. Take two plastic foam cups, and put about 1 inch of small rocks in the bottom of each one. Add 1 inch of sand to each cup on top of the rocks, and then add about 4 inches of potting soil to each cup.

Plant the six bean seeds, three in each cup. Water each cup to keep the soil moist but not wet. Put one cup in a sunny windowsill and the other in a dark closet. Check on your beans every day to see how they're growing. Are you surprised by the results?

What Happened? After several days, the plants growing on your windowsill will be healthy and green. The plants in the closet will be very pale, but they might be taller than the other plants. Plant cells have special light receptors. When they don't get enough light, they signal the plant to grow long and thin to seek out a light source. Since there's limited light, the plants in the closet don't produce the chlorophyll that makes the plants green and also absorbs sunlight to produce food. If you move the pale plants next to the green plants in the window, the pale plants will become green in time.

236 FROZEN COCOONS

What You'll Learn: Cocoons from certain kinds of moths can survive freezing temperatures.

What You'll Need: four cocoons; small jar; four large jars; marker; water

At the right time of year in your area, go out and gather four moth cocoons. Try to find cocoons that look the same and are from the same kind of moth.

Prepare five jars (one small jar and four large jars) by putting a few holes in each lid for ventilation. In the four large jars, add a branch with leaves from a plant that was growing near where you found the cocoons. Label two jars "FROZEN" and two jars "NOT FROZEN."

Put two cocoons in the small jar in your freezer. Put each of the other two cocoons in a large jar labeled "NOT FROZEN." After six hours, move the cocoons from the freezer into the two jars labeled "FROZEN." Store all four jars in a dark place. Once in a while, sprinkle the cocoons with just a few drops of water. Check the jars regularly. How many moths hatch? Are these moths able to survive freezing temperatures? Be sure to release any moths that hatch.

Extinction

Many groups of plants and animals have become extinct during Earth's history. Sometimes when plants or animals die, they leave behind impressions of their bodies in rock formations. We have learned much about extinct life-forms from these kinds of fossil remains.

SHELL PRINT

237

What You'll Learn: Using clay, you can see how a fossil print might be made.

What You'll Need: air-drying modeling clay; knife; pencil; small seashell; leather strip

Real fossils are formed in several different ways. They can be actual hard remains of ancient organisms, parts of organisms that have been replaced by minerals, or impressions of the organisms that have been preserved in the sediments. Using a shell and clay, you can imitate this process.

Start with a ⅜-inch-thick slab of air-drying modeling clay. Cut out a circle of clay with a 2-inch diameter. Use a pencil to poke a hole through the top of the clay circle. Press an interesting small seashell firmly into the circle of clay. Carefully remove the shell. It should leave a clear impression behind. The impression will resemble a fossil imprint. Allow the clay to air dry. Thread a leather strip through the hole, and tie the ends in a knot. You can wear your shell imprint around your neck.

LONG, LONG AGO

238

What You'll Learn: Earth has a very long history.

What You'll Need: reference books; roll of toilet paper; calculator; paper and pen

Scientists divide all of the time that has occurred since the formation of the Earth into eras. The three most recent eras are the Paleozoic era, which covers the time between 570 and 225 million years ago; the Mesozoic era, which lasted from 225 to 65 million years ago; and the Cenozoic era, which dates from 65 million years ago to the present. Use a reference book to find the dates of all the eras in Earth's history.

Get a roll of toilet paper that has 1,000 sheets. You will use this to represent the passage of time over Earth's history. Since the Earth is roughly 4.5 billion years old, each sheet of paper can represent 4.5 million years. To figure out how many sheets you need to represent each era in Earth's history, look in your reference books to find out how long each era lasted, and then divide that number by 4.5 million. Unwind the paper, carefully counting off each sheet, and mark each of the era boundaries. How much of the paper do you need to represent the amount of time humans have lived on Earth?

239 LIFE CHART

What You'll Learn: Geologic time periods have been given names, and different creatures lived during each period.

What You'll Need: reference books; poster board; markers; ruler

Find a geologic time chart in a reference book; check in encyclopedias or in books about dinosaurs or Earth's history. Use the information in the reference books to make a large chart on poster board. Give your chart five columns: "ERA," "PERIOD," "EPOCH," "MILLIONS OF YEARS AGO," and "CREATURES."

Down the first column, from top to bottom, print the names of three eras: "CENOZOIC," "MESOZOIC," and "PALEOZOIC." Using reference materials, complete the columns of your geologic time chart. For example, in the Period column for the Cenozoic, you will divide it into two periods: "QUATERNARY" and "TERTIARY." Under the Epoch column for Tertiary, you will print the names of five epochs: "PLIOCENE," "MIOCENE," "OLIGOCENE," "EOCENE," and "PALEOCENE." In the Millions of Years Ago column after Pliocene, you will print "5." Find one or two plants or animals that lived during each period, and draw them in the final column. A saber-toothed tiger, for example, might appear as a creature in the Quaternary Period.

Cells

Cells are the basic units of living things. Most cells consist of a small mass of protoplasm and a nucleus, all surrounded by a membrane. Cells are able to reproduce, they take in food and produce waste, and they usually perform a specific job.

THIRSTY SPUD

What You'll Learn: Living cells are able to absorb and pass on water.

What You'll Need: potato; knife; spoon; pan of water; sugar

Cut the ends from a potato, and discard them. Peel a 1-inch strip of skin from the bottom of the potato. Using a knife and spoon, scoop out a cavity about 1 inch deep in the top of the potato. Stand the potato up in a pan filled with water so that the peeled bottom is in the water. Put a spoonful of sugar in the cavity in the top of the potato. Let the potato stand in the water for 24 hours, and then check to see if any changes have occurred.

What Happened? The cells of the potato drew water up from the pan to the top of the potato. Individual cells took in water molecules from the water in the pan and passed them on to the cells above them in a process called *osmosis*.

SEE CELLS

What You'll Learn: Plant cells have specific shapes and structures.

What You'll Need: microscope with about 50-power magnification; a leaf with thin leaves, or an onion skin; glass slides; water; eyedropper (If you do not have your own microscope, you may be able to borrow one from your school.)

Set up your microscope on a table. Find a plant with thin leaves, such as elodea (a common freshwater aquarium plant), or use a piece of onion skin. Place a leaf on a glass slide. Add one drop of water, and place a cover slide over the leaf and water. Look at the slide under your microscope. You should be able to make out box-shaped structures. These are plant cells. If you look closely, you should be able to see tiny green parts in the cells. These contain chlorophyll, which gives the plant its color and helps the plant produce food.

242 TWO-HEADED TRANSPLANT

What You'll Learn: You can graft two similar plants together.

What You'll Need: knife; rubbing alcohol; two small, columnlike cactus plants of the same diameter; yarn; newspaper; cotton balls

Caution: *This project requires adult supervision.*

Dip a sharp knife into rubbing alcohol to sterilize it. Get two small, columnlike cactus plants in pots. Put a piece of yarn underneath each of the cactus plant pots; the yarn should be long enough so that the ends can be tied together at the top of the plant. Fold a newspaper into a thick pad, and use it to protect your hand while you handle the plants. Slice off the top of each cactus plant. Do not touch the cut surfaces of the plants.

Switch the tops of the two plants. Using cotton balls to protect your fingers, carefully press the new top onto the base of each cactus plant. Take the yarn under each pot, and securely tie the ends at the top of each plant to hold the new top in place. Put the pots in a sunny window. After a month, the grafts should heal, and you can remove the yarn from your plants.

What Happened? In time, each cactus produced new cells that joined together with the cells of the other cactus to heal the plant.

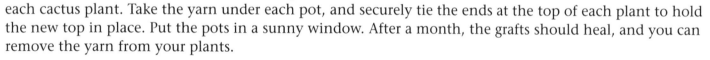

Sunlight, Water, and Air

Plants need sunlight, water, and air to thrive and be healthy.
Plants use light from the sun to convert carbon dioxide and water into food and oxygen in a process called *photosynthesis*. Plants also take other important nutrients that they need from the soil.

GROWING UP SIDEWAYS

243

What You'll Learn: Plants tend to grow toward the light.

What You'll Need: lima beans; water; two plastic cups; soil; a cardboard box with a lid; scissors

Soak four lima beans in a cup of water overnight. Put potting soil in two plastic cups, and plant two beans in each cup. Place both cups in a sunny window. Water the plants to keep the soil moist but not wet. When the bean plants are growing well and are about 3 inches high, cut a 3-inch hole in the side of a cardboard box. Set the box in the window so that the hole has sunlight shining on it. Leave one of the plants where it is, and put the other one inside the box. Continue to water the plants equally; keep the lid on the box closed except when you are giving the plant water. Observe the growth pattern of the two plants for a few weeks. Do you notice any differences?

What Happened? While the plant outside the box continued to grow straight upward, the plant inside the box turned toward the hole in the side of the box. The plant changed its growth pattern to reach toward the sunlight.

LIGHT AT NIGHT

244

What You'll Learn: Plants respond to increased light.

What You'll Need: lima beans; water; four flowerpots; small rocks; sand; potting soil; marker; fluorescent light

Soak eight lima beans in water overnight. Prepare four flowerpots for planting. Put 1 inch of small rocks in the bottom of each pot. Put 1 inch of sand over the gravel and 4 inches of potting soil over the sand. Plant two lima beans in each pot. Water to keep the soil moist but not wet. Label two of the pots "NIGHT LIGHT." Put all four pots in a sunny window by day. Put the two "Night Light" pots under a fluorescent light each evening, and put them back in the window with the other two plants each morning. Observe the growth of the plants over several weeks. Do the plants getting light at night grow faster than the other two?

245 HOTHOUSE

What You'll Learn: A greenhouse collects and stores heat.

What You'll Need: cardboard box; knife; ruler; pencil; newspaper; tape; aluminum foil; empty soup cans; water; plastic wrap; rubber bands; seedlings in pots; heavy plastic

Find a cardboard box about 14 inches deep, 10 inches high, and 12 inches wide, and cut off the top. Cut off one of the 10×14-inch sides of the box; this will be the front of your greenhouse. On both of the 10×12-inch sides, draw a line from the front bottom corner to the back top corner; cut along the lines so that you remove a triangular piece from each of the two sides. Cut one U-shaped flap in both sides; each flap should be 4 inches across and 1 inch high. By bending these flaps open or closed, you will be able to control airflow in your greenhouse.

Tape several layers of newspaper to the outside of the back wall for insulation. Tape a piece of aluminum foil to the inside of the back wall for a reflector.

Place the greenhouse in a sunny spot outdoors. Fill several empty soup cans with water, and cover the tops of the cans with plastic wrap held in place with rubber bands. Place the cans in a row against the back wall; they will help to store heat in your greenhouse. Put several seedlings in pots inside the greenhouse.

Tape a large piece of heavy clear plastic to the top of the back wall, and pull it over the top and front of the greenhouse; the plastic should be wide enough to cover the greenhouse and long enough to tuck at least 1 foot under the greenhouse. Lift this cover when you want to water your seedlings.

TEMPERATURE AND SEEDS

246

What You'll Learn: Temperature can affect how fast seeds germinate.

What You'll Need: three wide-mouthed jars; small rocks; sand; potting soil; flower seeds; refrigerator; pen and paper

Get three empty wide-mouthed jars, such as mayonnaise jars. Put 2 inches of small rocks at the bottom of each jar. Cover the rocks with 2 inches of sand. Then add 4 inches of potting soil.

Plant four of the same kind of flower seeds in each jar, following the directions on the package for the depth that the seeds should be planted. Put the three jars in different places: one jar in the refrigerator, one jar on top of the refrigerator near the back, and one jar near a cold garage wall. Water each of the jars occasionally so that the soil is moist but not wet. Observe the three jars each day, and write down what you see. Do the seeds in one of the jars germinate faster than in the others? What do you think caused any differences you observed?

 # CHILLY VEGGIES

247

What You'll Learn: Seeds will still germinate after being frozen.

What You'll Need: dried peas and lima beans; envelopes; freezer; four pots; rocks; sand; potting soil; marker; water

Put six dried peas and six dried beans in an envelope. Put the envelope in your freezer for two days. Put six dried peas and six dried beans in another envelope. Put that envelope in a drawer for two days.

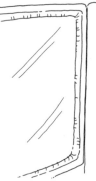 

Prepare four pots for planting. Put about 1 inch of small rocks in the bottom of each pot. Cover the rocks with 1 inch of sand, and cover the sand with 4 inches of potting soil. Label the pots as "FROZEN PEAS," "PLAIN PEAS," "FROZEN BEANS," and "PLAIN BEANS."

Plant your peas and beans in the appropriate pots. Water them to keep the soil moist but not wet. Put all four pots in a sunny window, and observe them for several weeks. Did the frozen seeds grow?

YEAST FEAST

What You'll Learn: A yeast plant can't make its own food.

What You'll Need: yeast; bowl; water; two glasses; measuring cup and spoon; sugar

Pour two packages of yeast into a small bowl. Add 1 cup of warm water, and stir to dissolve the yeast. Pour half of this mixture into one glass and half into another glass.

Mix 1 tablespoon of sugar into one of the glasses. Set both glasses in a warm spot, and check on them frequently. The one with the sugar will soon be foaming with bubbles.

What Happened? Yeast is a plant, but unlike green plants, it cannot make its own food. When you supplied food in the form of sugar, the yeast began to consume the sugar and produce carbon dioxide gas and alcohol. The foam is made up of bubbles of gas.

BUBBLE, BUBBLE

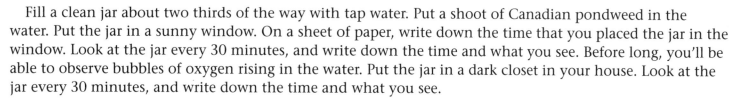

What You'll Learn: Plants give off oxygen as they make food.

What You'll Need: jar; water; Canadian pondweed; paper and pen; clock

Fill a clean jar about two thirds of the way with tap water. Put a shoot of Canadian pondweed in the water. Put the jar in a sunny window. On a sheet of paper, write down the time that you placed the jar in the window. Look at the jar every 30 minutes, and write down the time and what you see. Before long, you'll be able to observe bubbles of oxygen rising in the water. Put the jar in a dark closet in your house. Look at the jar every 30 minutes, and write down the time and what you see.

What Happened? While the plant was receiving sunlight, it was able to carry out photosynthesis. As a part of this process, the plant produced oxygen as a waste product, which made bubbles in the water. Without sunlight, the plant could not carry out photosynthesis.

FRESH AIR

250

What You'll Learn: Seeds need air to sprout.
What You'll Need: two glass jars with lids; dried peas; water

Fill two glass jars with dried peas. Add a little water to both jars, and put on the lids. Shake the jars to be sure that every pea gets wet. Take the lid off one jar, and leave the lid on the other. Put the jars side-by-side in a sunny window for several days. Add water as it evaporates from the open jar. Observe the peas every day to look for any changes.

What Happened? The pea seeds in the open jar sprouted, but the seeds in the sealed jar did not because they received no air. Seeds and plants need air to be able to grow.

 # WHO NEEDS DIRT?

251

What You'll Learn: You can grow a sweet potato plant without soil.
What You'll Need: toothpicks; sweet potato; glass; water

Insert three toothpicks around a sweet potato near the large end so they stick out to the sides in different directions. Fill a glass most of the way with water. Put the sweet potato into the glass small-end first, and rest the toothpicks on the rim so they hold up the sweet potato. There should be enough water in the glass so that about three quarters of the sweet potato is covered. Put the jar in a sunny spot for several days. Add water as needed. Soon you will have a beautiful vine growing from the top of the potato.

What Happened? Usually you put a plant into the soil to make it grow, but you can grow some plants without soil. When the sweet potato plant was growing with its roots in the soil and its leaves in the sun, it produced food through photosynthesis and stored carbohydrates in the potato. This stored food in the sweet potato provided the energy needed to grow a new plant.

252 WAY DOWN DEEP

What You'll Learn: The depth at which seeds are planted can affect how well and how fast they grow.

What You'll Need: empty aquarium; small rocks; sand; potting soil; corn seeds; black paper; tape; pen and paper; ruler; scissors; scale

Place 2 inches of small rocks in the bottom of an empty aquarium. Cover these with 2 inches of sand, and cover the sand with 8 inches of potting soil. Plant 16 corn seeds about 1 inch apart from each other in the aquarium; plant four of the seeds 1 inch deep in the soil, four seeds 2 inches deep, four seeds 4 inches deep, and four seeds 6 inches deep. Put the seeds near the glass wall of the aquarium so you can see them. Tape black paper over the outside of the glass to cover the seeds.

Water your seeds occasionally to keep the soil damp but not wet. Lift the paper to look at your seeds every day. Write down your observations and the date. Measure the length of roots and stems. Always tape the black paper back in place.

After six weeks, cut off the parts of each group of plants that are growing above the soil. Use a scale to weigh each group of plants. Based on the weight, what do you think is the best depth for planting corn seeds? Why do you think the depth of the seeds made a difference in how the plants grew?

253 HOW DOES YOUR GARDEN GROW?

What You'll Learn: Different types of soil can affect plant growth.

What You'll Need: four flowerpots; small rocks; garden soil; potting soil; vermiculite; sand; five potted marigold plants

Put about 2 inches of small rocks in the bottoms of four flowerpots. Fill one pot with soil from your backyard, one with potting soil, one with vermiculite, and one with sand; label each pot to indicate the soil it contains. Remove five marigold plants from their original pots, and gently rinse their roots. Plant one in each of the four pots you prepared, and return one to its original pot.

Keep the plants indoors in the shade for a few days to allow them to recover. Then put all five pots in a sunny window. Water them as needed on the same schedule to keep the soil moist but not wet. Which plants thrive and which do not? Which have the most blossoms?

What Happened? Plants get moisture and nutrients from soil. The growth of your marigold plants was affected by the kind of nutrients available in the different soils and by how well the soils held moisture.

Classifying Plants

Plants can be grouped, or classified, according to similar characteristics.
Scientists use very complicated classification systems based on things such as how
a plant reproduces or what parts it has. You can learn about classification by developing
your own systems for separating different plants into groups.

SEED HUNT

Visit a park, garden, or other planted area at the time of year when the plants growing there are producing seeds. Collect a few seeds from as many different plants as possible. Study each seed carefully. Does it have stickers or burrs that might get caught in animals' fur or in people's clothing? These stickers allow the seed to be carried from one spot to another. Is the seed inside a fruit that might be eaten by a bird or animal and eventually be eliminated by the animal in another spot? Does the seed have a parachute of some kind that enables it to fly? Classify your seeds by putting them into groups, perhaps based on how they are transported. Tape the seeds on sheets of paper labeled with the group names, and identify the plants they came from if you can.

SEEDS AND VEINS

Scientists divide most seed-making plants into two groups: *monocots* and *dicots*. The seed of a dicot has two halves, which are food parts and become the two first leaves of the plant. The seed of a monocot has only one part. These plants also differ in their leaves. Dicots have leaves with veins that look like nets with strands that cross over each other. Monocots have leaves with veins that run parallel to one another.

Collect leaves from a variety of plants: flowering plants, such as daffodils and poppies; trees, such as oak, maple, aspen, and hickory; vegetables, such as beans and corn; and different grasses, palms, and shrubs. Spread the leaves out on a table, and look carefully at the veining in the leaves. You may want to use a magnifying glass. Separate the leaves into dicots and monocots by the way the veins in the leaves look.

FLOWER-BY-NUMBERS

256

What You'll Learn: Plants can be classified by the types of flowers they produce.

What You'll Need: pen and paper; magazines; scissors; glue

Seed-making plants can be classified into dicots or monocots by counting the flower parts. Flowers that have their petals and stamens in groups of four or five are dicots. Flowers that have petals and stamens in groups of three, six, or nine are monocots.

Label one sheet of paper "DICOTS" and another sheet "MONOCOTS." Look through magazines for pictures of flowers. If the picture is clear enough, count the petals and the stamens sticking up from the center of the flowers. Cut each flower out, and glue it to the appropriate sheet of paper based on the number of petals and stamens it has. Identify as many of the flowers as you can by name.

YOU ARE WHAT WE EAT

257

What You'll Learn: You can classify plants according to the part of the plant that people use for food.

What You'll Need: pen and paper; magazines

Label a sheet of paper "ROOTS." Look through magazines for pictures of plants with roots that people use for food, and write the plant name on your paper. You might include radishes, carrots, and beets. What others can you find? Label another sheet of paper "LEAVES." Look for magazine pictures of plants to include on this sheet. Among them might be lettuce, spinach, and cabbage. What others can you find? Label a sheet of paper "SEEDS." Look for magazine pictures of plants to include on this sheet. You might include peas, beans, and nuts. What others can you find? Label a sheet of paper "FRUITS." Look for magazine pictures of plants to include on this sheet. You might include pears, peaches, apples, and grapefruit. What others can you find? What other sheets might you label and include in your classification system?

258 BARK PRINTS

What You'll Learn: Different trees have different patterns in their bark.

What You'll Need: paper; crayons

Bark is a very important part of a tree. It covers and protects the inner layers of the tree, and it plays a part in moving important nutrients from one part of the tree to another. Trees often have interesting patterns in their bark that can be used to tell one type of tree from another. Take a rubbing of a tree by holding a piece of paper up against the bark and rubbing over it with a wax crayon. You will capture a perfect impression of the tree's bark. Take rubbings of several different kinds of trees, and compare the patterns in the bark.

Food Chains

A food chain describes the connections between organisms that eat or are eaten by each other. A typical food chain has about 200 herbivores (plant eaters) for every one carnivore (meat eater). Some members of a food chain are producers, some are consumers, and some are decomposers. Producers make their own food. Consumers eat other organisms to get food energy. Decomposers break down waste products and decaying matter. A food web shows all of the connections between the food chains in one community.

SPINNING A FOOD WEB

259

What You'll Learn: You belong to a food web that includes many organisms.

What You'll Need: paper and pen; poster board; markers

As a human being, you are part of a food web. One night after dinner, write down the major components of each food item that you ate. Make a list of all the components, and write down where each one came from. Draw a picture of yourself at the top of a large piece of poster board. From left to right across the middle of the poster board, draw pictures of the plants and animals that provided your dinner, and draw a line from them to you. Think about where these organisms got their energy—from the sun, from certain plants, from other animals? From left to right at the bottom of the poster board, draw pictures of the energy source used by each plant and animal you ate for dinner. Look at all the different organisms you have on your chart. For each organism, think of two more organisms that have a food relationship with it—an animal that eats it or is eaten by it, or decomposers that break down the organism or its waste products. Draw these new organisms on your poster, and add lines to show the food relationships. Look at all the different creatures that you were connected to just by eating your dinner!

FISH KEEPING

260

What You'll Learn: An aquarium is a balanced ecosystem.

What You'll Need: aquarium; plants; fish; snails

One way to observe an ecosystem with producers, consumers, and decomposers is to set up a balanced aquarium. This requires quite a lot of equipment, some help from your local pet shop, and patience. Consult with an expert at your local pet shop about what you'll need to set up a balanced 10-gallon freshwater aquarium. Once the tank is ready, you can start adding creatures. Include snails to help keep the walls of your tank free from algae. Include a bottom scavenger to help keep the tank clean. Be sure to add fish that can live together, and don't overcrowd your tank. Follow directions for feeding. If you need brine shrimp for food, learn how to raise them yourself. Properly maintained, your aquarium will provide a lot of pleasure, and it will provide a good example of a balanced ecosystem with producers, consumers, and decomposers.

261 THANK MOO

What You'll Learn: People rely on cows for many food products.

What You'll Need: paper and pen

Visit a local grocery store, and look carefully through all the aisles. Try to find as many products that come from cows as you can. Look in the meat department and dairy department, of course, but check other places, too. Write down each type of food that you find. How many things are on your list?

CHAIN GAME

262

What You'll Learn: Each link in a food chain supports another link.

What You'll Need: markers; poster board; 3×5-inch index cards; dice

Design a game board based on a food chain. The path that you follow from Start to Finish might be along a river or a lake, through woods, or through a jungle. Draw a twisted path on the playing board, and design appropriate spaces on the board and pawns for the habitat you choose. If you choose a lake, for example, you might include a mosquito, a minnow, a large-mouth bass, and a human as spaces and as pawns. Some spaces will be colored and open. Mark several index cards "10 FOOD POINTS."

Players choose their markers, roll dice, and move the appropriate number of spaces. For example, if a player with the mosquito pawn lands on a human square, the player with the mosquito pawn gets a card and the player with the human pawn goes back to Start because mosquitoes bite humans. If a mosquito lands on a minnow square, the player with a minnow pawn gets a card, and the player with the mosquito pawn goes back to Start because minnows eat mosquitoes.

Continue the game until one player reaches the Finish space. Then have all the players add up the number of food points they have collected to see who has won.

MOLDY OLDY

263

What You'll Learn: Bread with preservatives in it will not spoil as fast as bread without preservatives.

What You'll Need: bread; resealable plastic bags; marker; napkins; water

Because bacteria can grow in food, many companies add preservatives to their food products to slow or prevent the growth of bacteria. In your grocery store, find loaves of white and wheat bread that contain preservatives. Also find loaves of white and wheat bread that do not contain preservatives. At home, mark four resealable plastic bags as follows: "WHITE WITH PRESERVATIVES," "WHITE WITHOUT PRESERVATIVES," "WHEAT WITH PRESERVATIVES," and "WHEAT WITHOUT PRESERVATIVES." Moisten four paper napkins, and put one in each of the bags.

Slightly moisten one slice of each kind of bread, and put them in the appropriate bags. Put all four sealed bags on a plate next to one another, and set the plate in a warm, dark closet. Check your bread slices each day. Where does mold start growing first?

BREAK DOWN

264

What You'll Learn: Microorganisms cause dead organic matter to decay.

What You'll Need: glass jar with a lid; fresh leaves and grass cuttings; water; pen and paper

Gather leaves and grass clippings, and pack them into a large clear jar. Add a few drops of water, and loosely screw the cap onto the jar. Be sure not to screw the cap tightly because gases will be given off that could break a tightly sealed jar.

Store the jar in a dark, warm place. Check on it every few days, and observe any changes. Write down your observations and the date each time you look at it.

What Happened? Microorganisms that feed on dead matter were able to grow in your jar. In feeding on the grass and leaves, they broke it down into a dark brown mixture that would, in the wild, become a part of the soil.

265 BEETLE TRAP

What You'll Learn: Some creatures consume parts of dead animals that they find on the ground.

What You'll Need: shovel; coffee can; food for bait; rocks

There are thousands and thousands of different kinds of beetles that live all over the world. Many of them are scavengers that move about at night looking for dead animals to consume. You might be able to trap one of these beetles, take a close look at it, and release it again.

With permission from your parent, dig a hole somewhere in your yard deep enough so that you can put a coffee can into the hole with its rim level with the ground. Put some food with a strong odor, such as cheese or tuna, in the can. Place the can in the hole. Put a small rock on the ground on either side of the can, and then lay a large, flat rock over the can, resting on the two small rocks. This "lid" will prevent someone from stepping in the hole, and it will also keep out rain.

Leave your trap in place overnight. Check it the next morning to see if you have caught a beetle. You might need to wait several nights or try different spots in your yard. Be sure to fill in any holes you dig and to release any beetles that you catch!

Animal Needs

All animals need certain basic things to survive. Although there is a lot of difference between a tiny shrimp that lives in the sea, a Canadian goose that flies high in the sky, and a huge lion that lives in Africa, all are animals that need food, water, shelter, air, and a community to live in.

MEALWORMS

266

What You'll Learn: A complete life cycle of a mealworm takes six months.
What You'll Need: mealworms; large container; cardboard; small container; mesh cloth; rubber bands; oatmeal or bran; apple or potato

Mealworms are the larval stage of the darkling beetle. They go through a complete life cycle in six months. To raise mealworms, you must meet their needs for food, water, shelter, air, and community.

Buy several dozen mealworms from a pet store or a biological supply house. Get a glass or plastic container about 10 inches across and at least 4 inches deep that they will use for shelter. Put 2 inches of oatmeal or wheat bran in the bottom of the container for food. Put an apple or potato in the container; the mealworms will use this as a source of water. Cover the container with a mesh cloth held in place by a rubber band; this will allow air to reach the animals. Lay a loose piece of cardboard on top to help keep in moisture.

The mealworms will develop into pupae. The pupae should be moved into another glass or plastic container with an inch of food in the bottom and covered with mesh cloth until they hatch into beetles. (If you leave the pupae in the large container, they may be eaten.) When the pupae hatch, return the beetles to the large container. The adult beetles will lay small eggs that will hatch into mealworms.

BIRD HAVEN

267

Imagine that you're going to set up the world's best bird habitat in your backyard. What would you need? Think of things that people use to attract birds to their yards, and think about the different resources that birds need to survive. Make your bird haven as complete as possible by filling as many of the birds' needs as you can. What kinds of ideas did you come up with for attracting birds? How would the birds use the resources you would provide for them? How would they fulfill these needs if you did not help them? Write down each of your ideas for attracting birds. Next to each one, write down the need that it fulfills. Do you have some of the same needs as the birds? Write down how you fulfill each of the needs that you share with the birds. If you can, use some of the ideas you came up with to make a real bird haven in your yard, and observe birds as they come to take advantage of your generosity.

ANT FARM

268

What You'll Learn: Ants work together as a community to survive.

What You'll Need: secure ant farm; blotting paper or sponge; ants; water; food scraps; pen and paper

Many animals live in a type of community. In an ant colony, some ants gather food, some care for the young, and a queen ant lays the eggs. If you capture ants, you may find only worker ants and not have a complete colony. But whatever ants you find will be interesting to observe.

An ant farm may be a tall, narrow frame of plastic or wood and glass, with a very fine mesh opening that admits air but will not allow ants to escape. Many ant farms are about 12 inches wide, 10 inches tall, and 2 inches deep. Inside, they contain sand and dirt that fills about two thirds of the space.

Once you have your ant farm and have purchased or captured ants, you can spend many hours in observation. The ants require little care. Put a piece of blotting paper or sponge in one side of the farm, and add water to this as needed. At the other side, add small amounts of different foods, and record the ants' reactions. You might try bread, syrup, sugar water, egg, cheese, lettuce, or a dead insect. Remove any food after two days if the ants are not eating it.

ANT PICNIC

269

What You'll Learn: Ants have food preferences.

Find an anthill somewhere in your neighborhood. Take several different kinds of food in small amounts: a spoonful of tuna, a spoonful of honey poured onto a leaf, a piece of an apple, a piece of lettuce, and a piece of a cookie. Place the different kinds of food in small piles that form a ring around the anthill about a foot away from its base. Stand back so that the ants don't crawl on you or bite you, and observe what happens. How do the ants find the food? How do they share it with each other? Do they seem to prefer one food over the other? Do they eat the food where they are or do they carry it away?

Individual Differences

Although organisms in a group may share many common traits, they will also be different in some ways. Kittens or puppies from the same litter often have different colors of fur or eyes, for instance. Animals in the same group can also differ in things like size. One may have better hearing than another, or have quicker reflexes. Recognizing individual differences is an important part of studying living things.

270 — ON THE RIGHT TRACK

What You'll Learn: Animals of the same species show differences in their tracks.
What You'll Need: old toothbrush; empty milk carton; scissors; paper clips; water; measuring cup; plaster of Paris; wooden stick

Go to a nearby park or other public place where people frequently walk their dogs. Find tracks left by dogs, and examine them closely. Count how many different sets of tracks you can make out. Select one footprint, and use an old toothbrush to brush away any debris in the track. Cut a strip about 1½ inches wide and 8 inches long from a milk carton; leave the bottom of the carton intact. Bend the strip into a circle, and hold the ends together with a couple of paper clips. Put your circle around the footprint.

Put 1 cup of water in the bottom half of your milk carton. Stir in 1 cup of plaster of Paris. Fill the collar around the animal's track to the top with the plaster, and smooth it with a stick. Bend a paper clip to make a hanger, and poke one end into the plaster. Let everything sit for 30 minutes. Be very careful when working with the plaster; it can be difficult to clean up. When the plaster is dry to the touch, peel away the cardboard. Lift up your mold of the track. After two hours, you can wash the plaster in running water. When it is dry, you can hang up the track by the paper clip hanger.

271 JUMPING CONTEST

What You'll Learn: Some grasshoppers are better jumpers than others.

What You'll Need: glass jar with lid; grasshoppers; paper and pen; tape measure

Catch several grasshoppers, and keep them in a large jar with holes poked in the lid. Place a large piece of paper on a flat surface outdoors. Put a grasshopper at the end of the paper. When it jumps, ask a friend to mark the landing spot. Measure the distance that it jumped. If possible, catch the grasshopper, and let it jump again. Take the average of its jumps. Repeat this with all of your grasshoppers. Did you find one that was an exceptional jumper? Be sure to release the grasshoppers back in the area where you found them.

PLANT COMPARISONS 272

What You'll Learn: Plants of the same species have individual differences.

Find two plants of the same species. You can use houseplants, plants from a vegetable garden, shrubs in your yard, or plants you find in the wild. Look at the two plants closely, and write down as many physical similarities as you can find between them. Look at things such as color, thickness of branches, shape of leaves, basic structure, and so on. Write "SIMILARITIES" at the top of a piece of paper, and write down all the things the two plants have in common. Now look at the plants to find ways that they are different. Look at the number of leaves, overall size, shape of branches, and anything else that occurs to you. Write "DIFFERENCES" at the top of another sheet of paper, and write down all the ways that the two plants are different from each other.

A SENSE OF BALANCE

273

What You'll Learn: Different things affect your sense of balance.
What You'll Need: paper and pen; 2×4-inch board; stopwatch

Use a piece of paper to make a chart with five columns. Label the top of the first column "NAME," the second column "EYES OPEN, LEFT FOOT," the third column "EYES OPEN, RIGHT FOOT," the fourth column "EYES CLOSED, LEFT FOOT," and the fifth column "EYES CLOSED, RIGHT FOOT."

Set a piece of 2×4-inch board in the middle of a carpet or lawn, making sure there is nothing nearby that might hurt a person who fell. Ask friends to stand on the board one at a time and balance on one foot, first the left foot and then the right foot. Use a stopwatch to time how long each person can keep their balance, and record the times on your paper. Then have your friends repeat this with their eyes closed. Do some people have a better sense of balance than others? Does having your eyes open or closed make a difference?

PULSE

274

What You'll Learn: Different individuals have different pulse rates.
What You'll Need: paper and pen; watch with a second hand

You may know that your pulse rate varies. After you exercise, for example, your heart beats faster. Pulse rates also vary from one individual to another. Do you think that younger or older people might have faster heart rates? Do you think that males or females will have faster heart rates? Is a person's pulse rate higher in the morning or evening? Write your answers down.

Draw five columns on a sheet of paper, and label them "NAME," "AGE," "SEX," "TIME," and "RATE." Ask friends and family members if you can test them. Put your first two fingers on the underside of the subject's wrist below the thumb. Count how many pulse beats you feel in 30 seconds, and multiply that number by 2. Record this on your chart, and fill in all the other information. Try to check each subject four times, twice in the morning and twice in evening. Does the information you gathered agree with your answers?

EYE SPY

275

Make the grid for a graph on a piece of paper. Up the left side, put the numbers 0 through 24, with 0 at the bottom left corner. Across the bottom of the sheet, list eye colors: "BROWN," "BLUE," "GREEN," and "HAZEL." On the school playground, at the swimming pool or park, or at some other place where you meet a lot of people you know, spend some time checking eye color. Write down each person's name and eye color. After you have checked 24 people, fill in your graph.

How many people had brown eyes? Draw a line to that number in the column above brown eyes. Color the column brown up to that number. Repeat this for the other three columns, coloring the blue eyes column blue, the green eyes column green, and the hazel eyes column gold. Among this group of friends, what eye color was most common? What color was least common?

BLOWHARDS

276

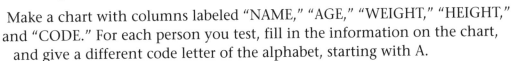

What You'll Learn: Lung capacity varies among individuals.

What You'll Need: paper and pen; water; large bowl; empty 1-gallon jug with a cap; plastic tubing; antiseptic wipes

Make a chart with columns labeled "NAME," "AGE," "WEIGHT," "HEIGHT," and "CODE." For each person you test, fill in the information on the chart, and give a different code letter of the alphabet, starting with A.

Pour about 3 inches of water into a large bowl, and set it on a counter. Fill a 1-gallon jug with water, and screw on the cap. Place the jug upside down into the bowl of water. With the top of the jug below water, remove the top, and slip a 3-foot length of clear plastic tubing into the jug.

Ask each subject to take a big breath and blow as much air as they can into the length of tubing. Mark the water level on the jug, and put the person's code letter by it. Wipe the tubing clean with an antiseptic wipe before another subject uses it. Compare the data you gathered from your test.

HUMANS: BODIES AND HISTORY

Human beings share many characteristics with animals, but we are also unique. Our bodies work in ways similar to other animals, and we have the same needs of food, air, shelter, and community. However, we are able to think in ways that no other creatures can, and we can create and use tools to shape much of our environment. In this chapter, you will learn about the way your body is built and about the ways we study our unique place in the world.

Muscles and Bones

Your body contains over 200 bones that are connected by strong tissues called *ligaments*. This skeletal system gives your body its shape. Working together with muscles, it also allows your body to move in different ways. The design of your skeleton and muscles influences how you are able to survive.

277 NEED KNEES

Joints are places where two or more bones meet, and you have them all over your body—neck, elbows, fingers, hips, knees, and ankles, just to name a few. Having joints makes your body more flexible and allows you to move. You use them every time you walk, jump, raise your arm, sit down, grab an object with your hand, or open your mouth. To get an idea of how important your joints are, try walking up stairs without bending your knees. You'll find that it is difficult or maybe even impossible. The shape of your knee and the way the bones move together allow you to bend your leg.

WING DING

278

What You'll Learn: The four bones of a chicken wing are designed to allow the chicken to flap its wings.
What You'll Need: chicken wing; pot; water; stove; fork

Caution: *This project requires adult supervision.*

Boil a chicken wing in water for about 20 minutes. Carefully remove the meat from the bones without pulling the bones apart from each other. Examine how the bones are held together. The connective tissues holding bones together are called *ligaments*. Observe the four bones in the wing. How are they different? How do you think a chicken's leg bones would be different from its wing bones?

SKELETONS IN THE CLOSET

279

What You'll Learn: Different animals have different skeletal structures.

What You'll Need: reference books

Look through a variety of reference books to find pictures of animal skeletons. Find as many different kinds of animals as you can. Look at the structure of the different skeletons. How are the bones arranged to give support in different animals? How are the bones arranged to allow movement in different animals? Try to make predictions about the different animals' diets and habitats and about how they live in general based on clues in their skeletons. If you can't be sure where an animal lives or what it eats, can you at least predict where it does *not* live and what it does *not* eat? Look in the reference books for information that will tell you whether or not your predictions were correct.

PIPE CLEANER BACKBONES

280

What You'll Learn: Some animals have backbones that run through the centers of their bodies.

What You'll Need: pipe cleaners; scissors; pictures of various animals

Use pipe cleaners to make skeletons of different animals. Start each skeleton by forming the backbone of the animal. Cut and bend pipe cleaners to make other bone parts (legs, heads, tails). Try to make a dog first. Then make other creatures, such as birds, dinosaurs, fish, or reptiles. You might want to try a giraffe or a human. Use pictures of the animals as a guide if that will help you.

HOLLOW STRENGTH

What You'll Learn: Long bones are hollow or filled with soft tissue, which helps them to be strong but light.

What You'll Need: paper; tape; paper plate; measuring cup; wooden blocks or other weights

Roll up a sheet of notebook paper into a tube about 1 inch wide. Tape the tube closed so it doesn't unravel. Repeat twice more so you have three paper bones. Stand the bones up on their ends. Put a paper plate on top of the three rolls. The hollow rolls support the plate! Now start adding wooden blocks to the plate. Count how many blocks the plate can hold before it collapses the bones. These bones are strong, so they might be able to hold quite a few blocks.

Roll three more sheets of paper as tightly as you can, so there is no hollow section. These bones use the same amount of paper, but they are much thinner. Stand them on end, and put the plate on top of them. Put blocks on the plate until these bones collapse.

What Happened? The hollow bones were able to support more weight. Having a hollow center gave them a better design and made them stronger. The large bones in your body are also hollow. This makes them strong, so they can support more weight, but light, so it takes less energy to move them.

DEBONING

What You'll Learn: Bones without calcium have less strength.

What You'll Need: chicken leg bone; vinegar; container with cover

Remove the meat from a chicken leg bone. Place the bone in a container, and pour in vinegar until the bone is covered. Put a lid on the container, and leave it undisturbed. After four days, remove the bone. Rinse it with water. Is the bone different than when you started?

What Happened? The acid in the vinegar dissolved the calcium in the bone. Without calcium, the bone lost its hardness and became weaker.

BREAKING BONES

283

Get part of the leg bone of a cow or sheep from a butcher. Ask the butcher to cut the bone in half near the middle of the leg so you can see what the inside looks like. Observe the characteristics of the bone. You will see that the bone is composed of a tough outer layer called the *periosteum.* Underneath this is the *compact bone,* which gives the bone strength. The center is either hollow or contains a soft area called the *marrow.* The insides are not solid because this would make the bone too heavy. Make sure you wash your hands after doing this activity.

GET A BACKBONE

284

What You'll Learn: The backbone is made of a column of bones called vertebrae.

What You'll Need: Seven small, twelve medium, and five large spools of thread; string; tape; balloon

The backbone is made of many bones called *vertebrae.* These are arranged in a line or column. To create a model of the human backbone, thread string through the center of several spools of thread, and tape the ends so they stay in place. Connect seven small spools to represent the cervical vertebrae at the top, connect twelve medium spools to represent the thoracic vertebrae in the middle, and connect five larger spools to represent the lumbar vertebrae at the bottom. Place a balloon (or ball) on the spools to represent a head. Notice how your model backbone can move in a variety of directions. In your model, string holds the vertebrae together. In a real backbone, ligaments hold the vertebrae together.

285 FLEX THOSE MUSCLES

What You'll Learn: Muscular contraction causes bones to move.

What You'll Need: cardboard; scissors; ruler; hole punch; brad; two rubber bands

Cut out two rectangles of cardboard about 7 inches long and 3 inches wide. Join the end of one piece of cardboard to the end of the other with a brad. Punch holes in the cardboard as indicated in the drawing. Cut two rubber bands, put them through the holes as indicated in the drawing, and retie them.

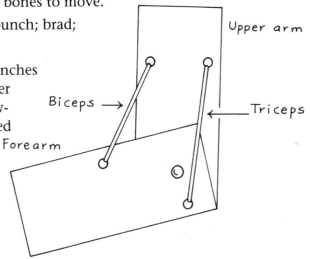

Make the arm move by pulling on the rubber bands. You'll see that pulling on one rubber band makes the arm bend and pulling on the other rubber band makes the arm straighten. Many of your muscles work in pairs like this, with one muscle pulling a bone in one direction and the other muscle pulling the bone in the other direction.

PROPORTIONAL DIMENSIONS 286

What You'll Learn: Many parts of your body are designed in proportion to each other.

What You'll Need: measuring tape or ruler

Measure the distance from your elbow to your wrist. Measure the distance from your elbow to your shoulder. These distances will be approximately the same.

Sway your hips back and forth, and find the top of your thigh bone. Measure from there to the top of your head. Now measure the distance from the top of your thigh bone to the bottom of your foot. These distances will be approximately the same.

Our skeletons play an important role in determining our size. Our body is arranged in proportions. Find other examples of things in proportion on your body.

Senses

Human beings have five senses: sight, taste, touch, smell, and hearing.
We rely on our senses to provide us with information about the world around us,
and they are some of the most important traits we have for survival.
Our senses also allow us to study the world and to enjoy it.

287 THE DOMINANT EYE

Normally when you look at something, each of your eyes captures an image of the object and sends it to your brain. Your brain then combines the two signals into one image, and that's what you see. This system makes you better at judging distances. However, your brain does favor one eye over the other. Stretch your arm out in front of you with one finger raised. Look at an object a few feet away, and line your finger up with it. Now close your left eye so that you're looking at the object and your finger only with the right eye. Now switch, closing your right eye and looking with your left. Closing one of your eyes will make it seem like your finger jumps over to the side so it is no longer lined up with the object. The eye that you close when this happens is your dominant eye. Your brain pays more attention to the image from that eye than it does to the image from the other eye. Have some of your family or friends do this test to see which of their eyes is dominant.

288 GOOD TASTE

What You'll Learn: We have taste thresholds for certain types of taste.

What You'll Need: measuring cup; 11 plastic cups; water; sugar; salt; paper towel; cotton swabs; paper and pen

Mix 1⅔ cups of water and ¼ cup of sugar to make a 12.5% sugar solution. Pour this in a plastic cup labeled "12.5% SUGAR." Add ½ cup of this solution to 1½ cups of water to make a 3.1% sugar solution, and label it "3.1% SUGAR." Add ½ cup of this to 1½ cups of water to make a 0.78% sugar solution, and label it "0.78% SUGAR." Add ½ cup of this to 1½ cups of water to make a 0.19% sugar solution, and label it "0.19% SUGAR." Make a series of salt solutions, following the above directions but using salt instead of sugar.

Rinse your mouth with water, and dry your tongue with a paper towel. Keeping the solutions out of your sight, have a friend place a clean cotton swab in one of the solutions and then put it on the middle of your tongue. Tell your partner if you can taste the solution and if it is sweet or salty. Your partner should write down whether or not you could taste the solution. Rinse your mouth and dry it, and have your partner try a different solution and record your response. Keep doing this until all the solutions are tested. Switch roles with your partner.

Which solutions could you taste, and which could you not taste? What was your threshold for sweet, and what was your threshold for salty? Was salt harder or easier to detect than sugar?

289 NO TASTE

What You'll Learn: The sense of smell is important for tasting food.

Next time you eat a meal, pinch your nose closed, and then taste the food. It does not taste as flavorful. Without the sense of smell, our tongues still detect sweet, sour, bitter, and salty tastes, but we don't detect the fragrance of the food. Fragrance plays a big part in how the food tastes. So next time you have to eat something with a taste you don't like, simply pinch your nose.

SHARP HEARING 290

What You'll Learn: Hearing ability varies among individuals.
What You'll Need: paper and pen; tape recorder; radio

Label a sheet of paper from 1 to 20. After every number, write a one syllable word, such as beat, park, broom, etc. Speaking at the same volume level, read your list into a tape recorder. Pause long enough after each word so that someone who heard the word would have time to write it down. Make a second list of different one-syllable words. Tape record this second list at the same volume level on your tape recorder.

Prepare two sheets of paper for each of four participants, and number each sheet from 1 to 20. Test the participants one at a time. Seat each person the same distance from the tape recorder. Turn on some soft background music on a radio. Then play the first recorded list of words. Ask each participant to write down the list of words he or she hears. Check them against your master list to see how many errors were made.

Repeat this procedure with the second list of words, but this time play the background music louder than before. After the participants write down the words, check to see if they made more or less mistakes when the background noise increased. Compare the results of the different individuals who took the test. Does someone in your group have the sharpest hearing?

291 RUNNING HOT AND COLD

What You'll Learn: If your brain receives a signal from a sense organ long enough, it will start to get used to it.

Caution: *This project should be done with adult supervision.*

Fill one jar with very hot water, one jar with warm water, and one jar with very cold water. Put one finger of your left hand in the hot water and one finger of your right hand in the cold water. Leave them in the water for a minute. Then put both fingers into the warm water at the same time. How does the water feel?

What Happened? You made one finger warm and the other cold, and your brain got used to them being that way. When you put both fingers into water of the same temperature, your brain got a different feeling from each of them.

Inheritance

All living things inherit their characteristics from their parents. Baby birds
have feathers and hollow bones because their parents passed those features on to them.
Baby fish have scales and gills because their parents passed those features on to them.
Baby humans are able to think complex thoughts because their parents
passed that feature on to them.

WE ARE FAMILY

292

We all have different physical features (unless we are identical twins); we have different eyes, hair, lips, hands, teeth, and fingers. Make a list of physical features, such as eye shape, skin tone, height (tall, medium, short), and so on. Compare yourself to a friend and then to your brother or sister. You probably have more physical characteristics in common with your brother or sister than you do with your friend. This is because we inherit our characteristics from our parents. We are similar to, but not exactly like, our parents. Each of our two parents contributes the genetic materials that design our bodies. We have some characteristics of our mother, some of our father, and some that are unique to ourselves.

LIKE MOM, LIKE DAD, LIKE ME

293

What You'll Learn: We have some characteristics of our mother and some of our father, but we are not exactly like either.

Compare yourself to your mother and father. Compare your hair, eye, and skin characteristics. Look at other traits, including how you act or speak. What are some characteristics you have from your mother? What are some characteristics you have from your father? Do you have any characteristics that are a blend of characteristics of your mother and father? Compare yourself to your grandparents in the same way, and compare your mother and father to your grandparents. Can you see traits that your parents received from your grandparents? Can you see any that you received from your grandparents?

294 GUPPY GENETICS

What You'll Learn: Guppy babies are usually different from each other and different from their parents.

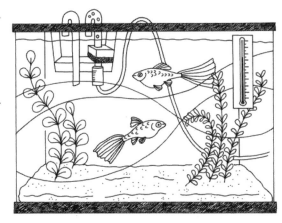

In this project, you will observe the babies produced by a female fancy guppy. Consult with an expert at your local pet shop about what you'll need to set up a balanced 10-gallon freshwater aquarium. This will require time, effort, and money. Put real or plastic plants in the tank so the babies will have places to hide.

Buy two pregnant female fancy guppies for your aquarium. Observe the females as they eat and their bellies get bigger. Keep watching them every day. One day you will notice that they are thinner and there are baby guppies hiding in many places in the tank.

As the babies grow older, compare them to each other. The more colorful fish are males, and the less colorful are females. Males also have longer fins. Compare the males with other males and the females with other females and with their mother. They may act differently. Their body color may be different. The fins or the tails may be different. Give different names to the fish, and make a chart that identifies some of the characteristics or behaviors of each fish, such as color, tail shape, aggressiveness, and so on. The young fish are different from each other and different from their mother, but they also share similarities. Allow the young fish to grow into adults, and observe their offspring.

THE GEEP

295

Scientists have successfully mated a species of goat with a species of sheep to produce what they call a geep. For a long time, people have bred donkeys with horses to produce mules. Mules have the intelligence of horses and the surefootedness of donkeys.

Find pictures of various animals in magazines or newspapers. Cut out the pictures of two species, and glue them together so they share body parts. Put your new animal on poster board. Give a name to your new organism. Make several new animals, and for each one, explain where it would live and how it would survive. Describe any advantages it would have over its "parents" and over other animals living in the same area.

Nutrition and Health

Our bodies depend on us to take care of them. Eating and exercising are two important ways that we give our bodies what they need. Learning more about food and exercise and how they affect us can help us do a better job of caring for our bodies.

296 NUT-RAGEOUS!

What You'll Learn: Food contains energy for our bodies.

What You'll Need: shelled nuts (walnut, pecan, cashew); needle; cork; metal cup; water; thermometer; matches; tongs; pen and paper

Caution: *This project requires adult supervision.*

Find different kinds of nuts that are about the same size. Stick one of the nuts on a needle, and stick the other end of the needle in a cork so it will stand by itself on a table. Put about ¼ inch of water in a metal cup. Measure the starting temperature of the water in the cup with a thermometer. Light the nut with a match. Using tongs, hold the cup over the flame. When the nut stops burning, record the temperature of the water. Compare that to the starting temperature to see how much the water's temperature increased. When the water cools to near its starting temperature, repeat with a different kind of nut. Which has the most energy?

What Happened? Nuts contain a great deal of food energy in the form of oils. When we eat nuts, our bodies take this energy and either use it or store it as fat. When you burned the nuts, their food energy was released as light and heat, which raised the temperature of the water.

READ THE LABEL

What You'll Learn: Different cereals may contain different amounts of nutrients.

Read the nutritional labels on cereal boxes. Make a chart that lists different vitamins, minerals, and nutrients down one side and lists the names of the cereals across the top. Put information from several types of cereals into your chart. Determine which has the most vitamin C for one serving. Which has the second most? Which has the least? Compare the cereals for the amount of iron they have and for other nutrients. Looking at all the nutrients, which cereals seem to be better for you? Make similar charts for other types of food.

WHAT'S THE SKINNY?

297

298

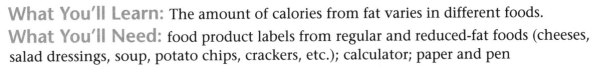

What You'll Learn: The amount of calories from fat varies in different foods.
What You'll Need: food product labels from regular and reduced-fat foods (cheeses, salad dressings, soup, potato chips, crackers, etc.); calculator; paper and pen

Calories are units of food energy. Look at the nutritional information on the food labels you have collected. Many of them will indicate what percentage of the food's total calories comes from fat. You can also calculate the percentage if you know the food's number of total calories and the number of calories from fat, which are usually listed on the label; divide the calories of fat by the total calories and multiply by 100%.

Using the food labels you've collected, compare the percentage of calories from fat for the regular food products and their reduced-fat versions. Calculate the percentage of how much the product has decreased in fat by dividing the original percentage by the reduced-fat percentage and multiplying by 100%. For example, suppose Paco's Tortilla Chips have 40% of their calories from fat, and Paco's Reduced-Fat Tortilla Chips have 20% of their calories from fat. Divide 20% by 40% and multiply by 100%; the result is 50%, which means the reduced-fat version of the tortilla chips has 50% less fat than the regular version.

PYRAMID POWER

299

What You'll Learn: Following the food guide pyramid can improve your diet.

What You'll Need: paper; marker; magazines; scissors; glue

The food guide pyramid shows the different food groups and how many servings of each we should eat in a day. Draw the pyramid on a large sheet of paper. Find photos in magazines of foods you like to eat. Paste the pictures where they belong in the pyramid. Let each picture represent one serving, and show the recommended number of servings for each group. For example, you should paste 3-5 pictures for the vegetable group. Compare the foods you eat in one day with your food guide pyramid. Should you make any changes in your diet?

DRIVE FOR FIVE

300

What You'll Learn: Fruits and vegetables are important parts of your diet.

Fruits and vegetables have a great deal of vitamins and nutrients that help people live healthier, longer, and more energetically. Experts on nutrition recommend that people eat at least five servings of fruits or vegetables each day.

Starting in the morning, write down the name of each fruit or vegetable that you eat during the day. A serving is roughly the size of an orange, ½ cup of cooked vegetables, ½ cup of canned fruit, or ¼ cup of 100% juice. Determine how close you came to eating five servings of fruits or vegetables during the day.

301 SUGAR BUZZ

What You'll Learn: Carbohydrates are absorbed into the blood at different rates.
What You'll Need: two glasses; corn syrup; red food color; measuring spoon; sugar; flour

Sometimes if you eat too much sugar, your head feels a bit odd and may start to hurt. Some people call this a sugar buzz. This also causes your body to work to remove the sugar from the blood. When all of the sugar is removed, your body is hungry again. Starches do not rush into the blood as quickly as sugar does.

Fill two glasses halfway with corn syrup. Add two drops of red food color to each glass to make artificial blood. Place 1 teaspoon of sugar on top of the blood in one glass and 1 teaspoon of flour on top of the blood in the other glass. Watch how long it takes for the blood to absorb the sugar and flour.

What Happened? The sugar is absorbed faster than the flour. The sugar is made of small molecules that dissolve faster than the large starch molecules in the flour. When we eat sugar, these small molecules quickly pass into our blood. When we eat starches, the molecules take longer to pass into our blood.

LARGE LUNGS 302

What You'll Learn: Blowing capacity varies from person to person.
What You'll Need: balloons; cloth tape measure; paper and pen

Caution: *Do not do this activity if you have asthma or any other breathing condition.*

Give identical balloons to several of your friends. Instruct each friend to blow up a balloon as much as possible with only one breath. Measure how big around everyone's balloon is with a tape measure, and write down the numbers next to your friends' names. Let the air out of the balloons, and repeat two more times. Take the average of the three tests. Who was able to blow the most air into their balloon? What is it about the person that enables him or her to do this? You may find that people who play musical instruments that require blowing, who do cardiovascular exercise, or who are large in size are able to blow harder.

303 HEART POWER

Our hearts beat constantly, 24 hours a day, without a rest. Close your hand into a tight fist. Your heart is about this size. See how long your hand muscles can work as hard as your heart. Look at a clock, and write down the exact time. Quickly open your hand, and stretch your fingers. Then quickly close your fingers into a tight fist. Open them and close them, open them and close them. Keep doing this until your hand is too tired. When you stop, look at the clock to see how long you were able to pump your hand. Your heart has to pump like that without stopping every second of every day. In one day, it beats 100,000 times and pumps 11,000 quarts of blood through your body.

STEP RIGHT UP! 304

What You'll Learn: Exercise increases your breathing rate and your heart rate.

What You'll Need: watch; paper and pen; stairs

Caution: *Do not do this activity if you have heart or breathing problems.*

Have a friend count the number of times you breathe in 30 seconds. Multiply this by 2 to get the number of times you breathe per minute. Record this number. Have your friend find your pulse and count the number of times your heart beats in 30 seconds. Multiply this by 2 to get the beats per minute. Record this number.

Stand at the bottom of a flight of stairs. Step up onto the first stair with your right foot and then with your left foot. Step down with your right foot and then with your left foot. Now step up with your left foot first and then your right foot. Step down with your left foot and then with your right foot. Continue stepping in this way for 30 seconds. Have your friend measure your breathing rate and pulse rate again. Compare these readings with the initial readings. How long does it take for these readings to return to normal?

What Happened? As you exercised, your muscles were working, so they needed more oxygen. Your breathing rate increased to get more oxygen in your body, and your heart rate increased to get that oxygen to your muscles.

Artifacts

Archaeology is the study of ancient people and civilizations. One of the ways we study ancient cultures is by examining *artifacts* that they left behind. Artifacts are any objects made by people for a specific purpose. By carefully examining artifacts, we can learn much about the people who used them.

NICKEL FOR YOUR THOUGHTS 305

What You'll Learn: Artifacts can reveal things about the people who use them.

Things people left behind are artifacts; these can be tools, clothing, food, or furniture. Suppose you were an archaeologist and you were researching an ancient culture. If you found only some coins, what things could you learn about the culture? Examine some nickels with a friend or relative. Think of questions you can ask and answer about the objects.

How were the objects made? How were they used? What do the words on them mean? Write down as many ideas as possible. For example, the coins tell you that this culture could melt and shape metals. They also tell you that the culture had a written language.

FIND THE ARROWHEAD

306

What You'll Learn: Artifacts can be found in different ways.

It can be difficult for archaeologists to find artifacts from other cultures. Often, the items are buried below the ground and require careful digging by many people. Sometimes they are buried by natural forces and then exposed by wind and rain centuries later. Other times, artifacts can be found in exactly the same spot they were left by the person who used them. Next time you are out in the woods or in another uncultivated area, look for rocks that have been shaped into arrowheads. These artifacts were made by Native Americans to use in their arrows for hunting and warfare.

 # SAND SEARCH

307

What You'll Learn: Archaeologists can use sound waves and rods to find materials buried underground.

What You'll Need: household objects; sand; 30 skewers or long sticks

Archaeologists sometimes use equipment to send sound waves into the ground, and then they study the reflections of the waves to find artifacts below the surface. They can also insert long rods into the ground to help them determine what is below the surface. Gather up a few items from around the house, such as cups, plates, and small garden tools. Have a friend or family member bury an object in sand. Have them show you where it is buried, but don't let them tell you what the object is. Now sink a skewer into the sand so it just touches the object. Leave the skewer in the sand. Do this with about 30 skewers. Try and guess the shape of the object. Then guess what the object is. After you guess, carefully dig up the object to see if you are right. Then bury an object for your friend or family member to identify.

308 MOVING ARCHAEOLOGY

What You'll Learn: The things people own give clues about how they live.

Visit a moving sale or an estate sale with an adult, and look over the items being sold. Try to determine as much as you can about the people who own the sale items. For example, if they have lots of pet care products, you might conclude that they are pet lovers. If they have lots of sports equipment, you might conclude that they are athletic. You can't be sure about your conclusions, but this is how archaeologists work. They draw conclusions based on what they find and then seek more facts to see if their conclusions were correct.

OLD AGE HOME 309

Working with an adult, identify the oldest object in your home that was made by people. This could be furniture, tools, letters, jewelry, photographs, or paintings. Once you have found the oldest item, try to answer some questions about it. What is the purpose of the object? Is it still used for the same purpose? When do you think it was made? Who originally owned the item? What can the object tell you about the original owner?

TRASH TALK

310

What You'll Learn: People's garbage can provide clues about how they live.

Caution: *This project requires adult supervision; be careful of any sharp or otherwise dangerous objects you might find.*

With an adult, go through your family's garbage. If you were an archaeologist who didn't know your family, what conclusions would you make? You might guess the kinds of food your family eats or the appliances your family uses to cook. You might make conclusions about family members' hobbies or about work projects done around the home. Archaeologists often analyze the trash of ancient civilizations to learn more about their culture.

TIME CAPSULE

311

What You'll Learn: Time capsules help people in the future understand past cultures.

What You'll Need: various objects; resealable plastic container; plastic bag; shovel; paper and pen

Gather objects that represent the current year. These can be baseball cards, newspapers, magazines, fashion items, or anything else you can imagine. You might write a letter that tells about yourself, your family, or your community. Put these items into a plastic container, and seal it securely. Put the plastic container into a plastic bag, and tie the bag closed.

Find someplace to bury the time capsule; make sure you have permission to do so. Dig a 3-foot hole in the ground, put your time capsule in, and cover it with dirt. Make a sign, and put it on the ground above the capsule, or make a map to the capsule. On your map or sign, indicate what year the time capsule should be opened. When it is opened, people will find artifacts that will give them some information about how you lived.

Human Tools

The most common artifacts found by archaeologists might be tools. Tools are a part of technology; they make work easier or more precise. While a few other animals are known to use simple tools, humans create and use tools in a much more sophisticated way than any other creatures do.

TOOLING AROUND

312

Imagine you are stranded on a deserted island. All you have with you are the clothes you are wearing, a small hunting knife, a book of matches, and a compass. It could be days, weeks, even months before you are rescued. Make a list of all the items you need to survive and of tools that will help you. For example, you need to eat and drink. Will you hunt, grow, or gather your food—or a combination of all three? What tools do you need to hunt, grow, or gather? Where will you find water, and how will you carry it and store it? Remember, you only have the items you were stranded with—all other tools you have to make from objects already on the island. If you are unsure what objects would be on an island, ask an adult. Since you have no idea when you will be rescued, you need to prepare yourself for a long stay. For example, what will you do when you run out of matches? You can turn this experiment into a game to play with your friends. Pretend the group of you are stranded and need to set up your own community. Will you have a government or laws? Will you trade with each other or have a system of money? How will you divide up the work?

TOOL TALLY

313

What You'll Learn: People rely on a variety of tools every day.

You use a number of tools every day. Every time you use a tool, take a minute to write it down on a sheet of paper. You might easily recognize some items as tools, such as hammers or scissors or spoons. However, you may not realize that some things you use every day are tools, such as your toothbrush, your bicycle, your lunch box, and even the pen you're using to write. At the end of the day, count up the number of tools you have used. Think about what life would be like if you didn't have some of these tools available to you. Which of the tools on your list did people have 100 years ago? What about 1,000 years ago? For the tools they didn't have, what did they use instead?

BUILDING BRIDGES

314

What You'll Learn: Bridges are used to cross over valleys, waterways, or roads.

What You'll Need: magazines and reference books; toothpicks; glue

Find pictures of several different bridges, either in magazines or in reference books. Study the pictures carefully. What do they have in common? In what ways are they different? Do some of the designs seem stronger than others? Using toothpicks and glue, build a simple bridge that can cross a 5-inch span. Test your bridge to see how much weight it will support by resting different objects on top of it. Can you think of ways to change your bridge's design so it will be stronger?

315 CLAY KITCHEN

What You'll Learn: Clay can be used to make a variety of tools for eating.

Using clay, try to make as many eating tools as possible. Make a list of all the tools you made. If you can't make a specific tool (for example, a fork), try to make a substitute tool that will have the same function. You will find out that clay is a very useful material for making many kitchen tools. Before people were able to work with metal, they often used clay to make tools and household items.

CLAY POT REFRIGERATION 316

What You'll Learn: Porous ceramic pots can keep their contents cool.
What You'll Need: unglazed clay flowerpot; cork or silicon sealant; plastic container; measuring cup; water; two thermometers; pen and paper; clock

This activity works best if done on a hot day. Seal the hole in the bottom of a clay flowerpot using either a cork or silicon sealant. Fill the pot with warm water, and add the same amount of warm water to a plastic container of about the same size as the pot. Measure the water temperature in each container, and write it down. Record the temperature every 20 minutes.

What Happened? You'll find that the water in the clay pot has a lower temperature than the water in the plastic pot. You'll also find that the water level drops in the clay pot but not in the plastic pot. The clay pot is porous; it allows water to slowly seep from the inside of the pot to the outside of the pot. When it reaches the outer part of the pot, the water evaporates, which cools the pot. People have used this method of refrigeration for thousands of years.

STICK RAFT

What You'll Learn: A raft can be made by tying sticks together.

What You'll Need: sticks; string; large container; water; various small objects

Gather some small sticks, and lay them side by side. Tie the sticks together securely so they make a raft. Put the raft in a container of water to see if it floats. Add some small objects, such as toy soldiers, washers, marbles, or paper clips, to see if your raft is able to support them. How many objects can the raft support before it sinks? Design a raft that will hold more objects. Rafts were one of the first types of boats people ever made.

FOIL FLEET

What You'll Learn: The design of a boat will affect how well it can perform.

What You'll Need: aluminum foil; scissors; large container; water; various small objects

Cut out four 6×6-inch squares of aluminum foil. Fold them into different shapes that will float on water. Put your boats in a container of water to see if they float. Add some small objects, such as toy soldiers, paper clips, or washers, to see if the boats support them. How many objects can each boat support before it sinks? Which boat holds the most? Design boats that will hold more objects.

THE INCREDIBLE UNIVERSE

Our Earth is one planet orbiting around one star—the sun. In the vast reaches of space, billions of other stars also shine, and some may have planets that orbit around them, too. But as far as we know, Earth remains the only place that supports life. In this chapter, you will explore the universe, the stars, the sun, and the moon. You will also look at the Earth and the many forces that shape it.

Constellations

In big cities, people have difficulty seeing the beauty of the night sky because of all the artificial light shining into the atmosphere. When city people visit the country, they often gasp when they see the view of the night sky on a clear night. Ancient people had a wonderful view of the night sky, and they spent a great deal of time studying the stars. They remembered stars by thinking of the groups of stars as representing gods or things on Earth. These groups of stars are called *constellations*.

TWINKLE, TWINKLE

319

What You'll Learn: Stars appear to twinkle when their light passes through Earth's atmosphere.

Look into the night sky, and focus your eyes on a star. Observe how the light seems to become slightly brighter and dimmer at times. The star appears to be moving, slightly left to right, slightly up and down. But the light the star gives off is fairly constant, and the star is not making any rapid movements. The twinkle effect occurs as light from the star strikes molecules in our atmosphere. These molecules cause the light to make small changes in its path.

STAR LIGHT, STAR BRIGHT

320

What You'll Learn: Some stars appear to be brighter than others.
What You'll Need: cardboard; scissors; ruler; colored cellophane; tape

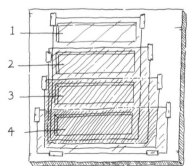

Cut four 1×4-inch rectangles next to each other on a piece of cardboard. Tape one sheet of cellophane over all four rectangles. Then tape cellophane over the last three rectangles. Then tape cellophane over the last two rectangles and finally over the last rectangle only.

View the night sky with your brightness detector. Notice you can see more stars when you look through fewer cellophane sheets. Only the light from the brightest stars is able to penetrate all four sheets. Try to find a star that you can see with one sheet but not with two sheets. Call this a one star. Find a star you can see with two sheets but not three. Call this a two star. Find a star you can see with three sheets but not four, and call this a three star. Any star you can see through all four sheets is a four star. Which type of star can you find most often? A star's brightness on Earth depends upon two things: the amount of light the star is putting out and how far it is from Earth.

321 SPECK-TRAL STARS

What You'll Learn: Constellations are groups of stars in the sky. They are often given names based on their shape.

What You'll Need: newspaper; white paper; paint; paintbrush; pencil

Thousands of years ago, people noticed the groups of stars and gave them names based on the shapes they seemed to form. Pegasus the Horse, Orion the Hunter, and Ursa Minor the Little Bear all got their names this way. Often, different cultures gave the groups their own names. What we call the Big Dipper, the Vikings called the Wagon, the Chinese called the Emperor's Chariot, and the English called a Plow.

Spread some newspaper over the floor or over a table. Place a sheet of white paper in the middle of the newspaper. Dip a paintbrush into paint. Hold the brush over the paper, and tap your hand so small paint specks fall on the paper. Think of these as stars, and examine them for patterns or shapes you recognize that could be constellations. Connect the paint specks with a pencil to form shapes you can recognize. Then paint more detailed pictures of the image. Write names for your constellations.

PLANETARIUM PRESENTATIONS 322

On one end of shoe box, cut a hole just big enough for a flashlight to fit into. Cut a rectangle out of the other end of the shoe box. Draw dots on a piece of paper to represent the stars of a constellation, and poke holes through the dots with a pin; do this for several different constellations. Put one of the sheets over the rectangular hole in the box, and tape it in place. Support the flashlight with a stack of books, and put it into the hole in the other end of the box. In a darkened room, turn on the flashlight, and project your constellation onto a wall. Quiz your friends or family to see if they can identify the different constellations.

MAP OF THE STARS

323

What You'll Learn: A star's position in the sky changes throughout the year.

What You'll Need: star charts (available in bookstores, science stores, and hobby shops, or on World Wide Web sites, such as "Star Facts" at: http://ccnet4.ccnet.com/odyssey

The patterns of stars remain the same, but their positions in the sky change. Star charts help us find constellations in the sky.

Bring a star chart outside on a clear night. Set the chart to the correct date and time. Hold the chart in front of you as you face north. Look at the chart and sky to see if you can find constellations. Find the Big Dipper and the Little Dipper. At the end of the handle of the Little Dipper is the North Star. Another way to find the North Star is from the Big Dipper. The part of the cup away from the handle is made of two stars. Start from the bottom star, and follow an imaginary line to the upper star. This will point you to the North Star. The North Star is important in navigation because it can always be used to identify which direction is north. All the other stars seem to rotate around this star.

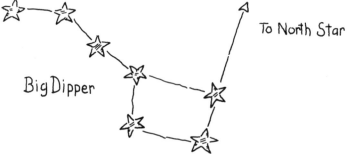

North Star

Little Dipper

Big Dipper

To North Star

324 HAPPY TRAILS

What You'll Learn: Circular star trails are produced on film when a camera shutter is left open and pointed at the night sky.

What You'll Need: time-exposure camera

On a clear night, set up your camera on a tripod so that it points toward the North Star. Open the camera to its widest aperture, and set the shutter to be open for two hours. When you develop the film, you will see that the stars' positions in the sky have changed. Streaks of light show their path. This is a result of the Earth's rotation. You'll see also that the star streaks on the film all circle around the North Star.

STAR MAP

325

What You'll Learn: A constellation's position in the sky changes as Earth rotates.

Find a place outside where you can see the sky from the southeast to the southwest and where you can also see several landmarks on the horizon, such as buildings or trees. Draw the view of the horizon with the landmarks on a sheet of paper. Mark the exact spot you are standing in so you will be able to find it again. When night approaches, stand in that spot again, and look for a constellation or group of stars in the southern sky. Put a dot to represent the group on your landscape map, and write the time next to it. Every hour for the next three hours or more, return to the spot, and mark the time and the group's location on your map.

What Happened? The stars moved in the sky due to the rotation of the Earth. Some constellations may even go out of view as the night progresses. Just as the sun seems to rise in the east and set in the west due to the Earth's rotation, stars show the same apparent motion.

UMBRELLA ASTRONOMY

326

What You'll Learn: The stars in the sky rotate around the North Star.

What You'll Need: white chalk; black umbrella; star chart

Using a piece of white chalk, draw a circle to represent the North Star on the inside of an umbrella around the central rod. Using a star chart for reference, draw one or more constellations on your umbrella. Now slowly turn your umbrella in a counterclockwise direction. The constellations seem to turn, but the North Star seems to stay in one place. When we view stars from Earth, they also seem to rotate around the North Star. This is caused by the Earth's rotation on its axis. The constellations rotate around the North Star once every 24 hours.

DIP INTO THE SEASONS

327

What You'll Learn: The positions of stars change from month to month.

Every month the stars in the sky rotate by one twelfth of the way across the sky, sort of like every 60 minutes the hour hand on a clock moves one twelfth of the way around the clock. Go outside at 9:30 P.M. Find the Big Dipper, and note where it is in relation to the North Star. Record the season. Do this for the other three seasons of the year.

What Happened? The Big Dipper's position around the North Star changed during the different seasons. The drawing shows the constellation's approximate positions for the different seasons at 9:30 P.M.

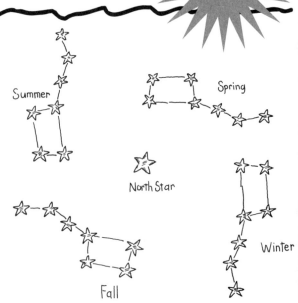

Earth's Rotation

The Earth's rotation on its axis is responsible for producing night and day. When one side of the Earth receives sunlight and experiences daytime, the other side gets no light and experiences nighttime. The sun's position in the sky can be used to tell what time it is during the day.

328 SUN TIME

What You'll Learn: The position of the sun in the sky can be used to tell time.

What You'll Need: clay; stick; watch or clock; chalk

Mold a piece of clay so that it will make a firm base. Put a stick into the clay so that it will stand upright. Put the stick on a blacktop or concrete surface where it can get light all day. Starting in the morning, draw a chalk line over the shadow of the stick at the start of each hour. Label the time near the line. Do this throughout the day. When you're done, you'll have a sundial that can be used to tell time. At any time during the next day, you can go look at where the stick's shadow falls, and tell what time it is by comparing it to the chalk marks you made. The sun's position in the sky changes gradually as the year goes on, so you'll need to reset your sundial each month by redrawing the chalk markings.

LIGHT/NIGHT

329

What You'll Learn: The Earth's rotation produces day and night.
What You'll Need: globe; flashlight

Turn on a flashlight, and place it on a table in a darkened room. Hold a globe of the Earth a few feet from the flashlight in its beam. Notice that half of the globe is lit up and half is dark. The dark side is night, and the light side is day. Rotate the globe clockwise, and watch how different parts of the world receive light and then fall into darkness. Can you see why the sun seems to rise in the east and set in the west?

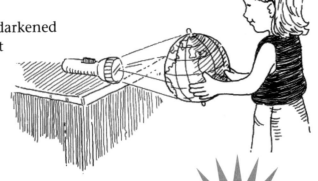

GLOBE TROTTERS

330

What You'll Learn: The amount of light reaching a hemisphere makes summer warm and winter cold.

Put a lamp in the middle of the room. Hold a globe about 5 or 6 feet from the lamp. Notice that the globe is tilted along its poles. This shows how the Earth is tilted. Hold the globe upright, and position it so the North Pole tilts away from the light source. Observe how the light falls on the Northern Hemisphere (above the equator) and on the Southern Hemisphere (below the equator). You can see that the Southern Hemisphere gets more light. If the Earth was in this position in its orbit, it would be summer in the Southern Hemisphere and winter in the Northern Hemisphere. Walk around the lamp in a circle, but move the globe as you walk so that the North Pole continues to point in the same direction. Notice that the way the light falls on the hemispheres changes as you walk around the lamp. When you're standing on the opposite side of the lamp, the Northern Hemisphere gets more light than the Southern Hemisphere. If the Earth was in this position in its orbit, it would be summer in the Northern Hemisphere and winter in the Southern Hemisphere.

331 HOURS IN A DAY

What You'll Learn: A day is 24 hours long, but the amount of daylight in each day changes throughout the year.

Keep a journal that records the hours of daylight in each day. Each morning if you are awake, record the time the sun rises. At the end of the day, record the time the sun sets. If you cannot observe the sunrise or sunset, check the times each day in the newspaper or on the radio. You will find that the days are shorter in winter than in summer. The longest day of the year is the summer solstice (around June 21), and the shortest day of the year is the winter solstice (around December 21).

SUNDIALS: OLD AND NEW 332

What You'll Learn: There are a variety of structures for sundials.
What You'll Need: Internet access to the World Wide Web

Check out World Wide Web sites devoted to sundials. Do a search on the words "sundial" and "time," and then check out the sites. Sites can change from time to time, but here are some interesting sundial Web sites you might be able to find.

The Richard Swenson Sundial is not only a functional sundial, but a modern work of art. To see this creation and to read the history of sundials, go to:
http://www.uwrf.edu/sundial/
For more pictures of modern dials, see:
http://www.ph-cip.uni-koeln.de/~roth/sonnenuhr.html
Of course, sundials have been around for a long time. To see ancient sundials, select Orologi Solari in the Astro Gallery at:
http//www.mclink.it/mclink/astro

The Moon

The moon is the closest astronomical object to our planet. Because it is so close, we know a great deal about it. People have studied it carefully for centuries, even when the technology for space observation was limited. The moon is also the only object in space that people have ever visited.

333 HEAD, BALL, MOON

 What You'll Learn: We sometimes see only a slice of the moon lit up because of our angle of view when we look at the moon.

Next time you are outside and you can see the moon during the day, get a big ball, like a basketball or a soccer ball. Stand in a sunny spot, face the moon, and hold the ball in front of you as if you were giving it to the moon. Your head, the ball, and the moon should all be lined up. Look at how the sunlight is shining on the ball. Although half of the ball is lit up, you can only see a portion of the lit ball. Now look at the moon. The portion of the ball you see lit up is the same as the portion of the moon that is lit up.

334 THE HULA BALL

What You'll Learn: The moon appears to change shape as it orbits around the Earth because of the way it is lit by the sun.

What You'll Need: table tennis ball; glue; string; hula hoop or cardboard ring; lamp

Glue a table tennis ball to a piece of string. Tie the string to a hula hoop. Turn off all the lights in the room except one lamp. Face the lamp, and stand in the middle of the hula hoop so the ball is between you and the lamp. The lamp represents the sun, the ball represents the moon, and you are the Earth. You can't see the lit side of your moon. This is called a new moon. Now turn your body and the hula hoop one-eighth of the way to your left. Watch how the light falls on the ball. You should see a crescent. Keep turning your body and the hula hoop, and watch how the light on the ball changes. When you have your back to the lamp, tilt the hula hoop upward so you don't block the light to the ball. This position represents a full moon. Continue rotating around, and watch as the moon wanes until you can no longer see the part of the moon that is lit up. This is a new moon again. You have just duplicated the phases of the moon as it orbits the Earth.

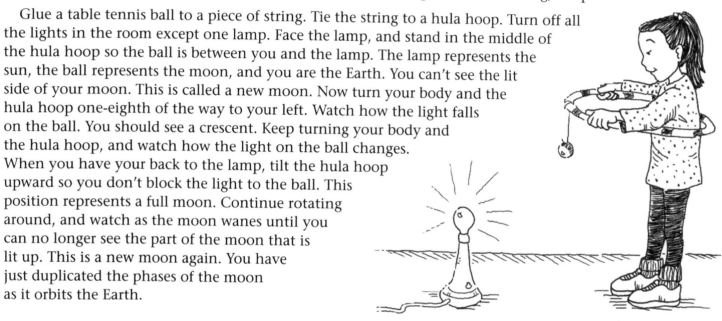

MOON MAP

335

What You'll Learn: The moon appears to change shape as it orbits around the Earth and is lit by the sun.

Find a place outside where you can see the sky from the southeast to the southwest and where you can also see several landmarks on the horizon, such as buildings or trees. Draw the view of the horizon with the landmarks on a sheet of paper. Mark the exact spot you are standing in so you can find it again.

You are going to plot the moon's position and its image every day for one month. You may wish to start on a night with a full moon or a new moon. At the same time every night, observe the moon from the spot where you drew your map. Draw the moon's position on the map, and write the date inside it. On a calendar, draw what the moon looks like in the square for that day. As the month goes on, you will see how the moon changes position in the sky and how the part of the moon that is lit by the sun changes.

BE THE MOON

336

What You'll Learn: One side of the moon always faces away from the Earth.

Have a friend stand in the middle of the room. Stand a few feet away, and face your friend. Walk in a circle all the way around your friend, but always keep your face toward him or her and your back away from him or her, so that your friend sees your front but never your back.

The moon circles the Earth in the same way. It makes one revolution in 27⅓ days. But it also rotates on its axis once every 27⅓ days. Thus, it always has the same side facing the Earth.

337 I'LL BE BACK

What You'll Learn: The terminator is the point on the moon (or on any planet) where day and night meet.

What You'll Need: binoculars or telescope

Focus binoculars or a telescope on the moon. Find the terminator, which is the line where day meets night on the moon. The lighting near the terminator makes it a great area for observing structures on the moon. Can you see any mountains or valleys?

BOXED MOON 338

What You'll Learn: The moon appears to change shape as it orbits around the Earth and is lit by the sun.

What You'll Need: shoe box; scissors; flashlight; spool of thread; glue; tennis ball; books

Cut a hole in one end of a shoe box big enough for a flashlight to fit through. Then cut eight peep holes around the box as indicated in the drawing. Glue a spool of thread to the center of the bottom of the box. Glue a tennis ball on top of the spool. Prop the flashlight on a stack of books, and shine its light through the hole. Look at the image of the moon from the eight different peep holes around the box. What does the moon look like from each peep hole?

What Happened? As you look at the ball from different angles, different parts of it will appear to be lit up. Our view of the moon changes in the same way. The amount of sunlight hitting the moon does not change throughout the month (unless there is a lunar eclipse, which is rare). Our view of the moon changes because we see it from different angles as it orbits around the Earth.

HULA HOOP ECLIPSE

339

What You'll Learn: Solar eclipses are caused by the moon blocking light to the Earth. Lunar eclipses are caused by the Earth blocking light to the moon.

What You'll Need: table tennis ball; glue; string; hula hoop or cardboard ring; lamp

Glue a table tennis ball to a piece of string. Tie the string to a hula hoop. Turn off all the lights in the room except one lamp. Face the lamp, and stand in the middle of the hula hoop so the ball is between you and the lamp. The lamp represents the sun, the ball represents the moon, and you are the Earth. Watch how the light falls on the ball. Turn your body and the hula hoop, and watch how the light on the ball changes. When you are facing the lamp, notice how the ball puts a shadow on your body. This is what happens during a solar eclipse. If you were standing on the Earth where the moon's shadow fell, you would be in the moon's shadow, and it would seem as if the sun had been covered. Continue rotating around until you have your back to the sun. Now your body blocks light to the ball. During a lunar eclipse, the shadow of the Earth makes it seem as if the moon has been covered.

 # VIEWING A SOLAR ECLIPSE **340**

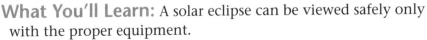

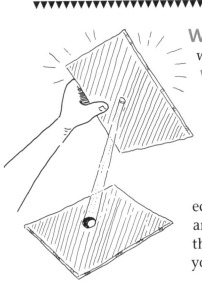

What You'll Learn: A solar eclipse can be viewed safely only with the proper equipment.

What You'll Need: two sheets of thin cardboard (or thick paper); pin

Caution: *Never look directly at the sun during an eclipse or any other time.*

Solar eclipses don't happen very often, but when they do, they are exciting. The newspaper and television stations will inform you when one will occur in your area. Total solar eclipses will occur on March 9, 1997, and on February 26, 1998.

You can never look directly at the sun, as it will damage your eyes. To view an eclipse, make a pinhole in a thin cardboard sheet. Line up the pinhole with the sun, and put another sheet of cardboard beneath it. An image of the sun will shine through the hole and appear on the bottom sheet. During an eclipse, if you keep your eye on the bottom sheet, you will be able to see the moon move across the sun.

341 UNDERSTANDING TOTALITY

What You'll Learn: A total eclipse occurs when a shadow, called an umbra, falls on a region of the Earth.

What You'll Need: big ball, such as a soccer ball; flashlight; books; small ball, such as a tennis ball; string; tape

In a dark room, put a large ball, such as a soccer ball, on a table. Then put a flashlight on a stack of books so that the light beam shines on the middle of the ball. Tape a string to a smaller ball, such as a tennis ball, and hold the smaller ball in the path of the light to make a shadow on the larger ball. This will be a model of a solar eclipse, where the large ball is the Earth, the small ball is the moon, and the flashlight is the sun.

If you hold the ball at the right distance, you will see a very dark shadow on the large ball surrounded by a lighter shadow. The dark shadow is called the *umbra,* and the lighter shadow is called the *penumbra.* If you were in the spot on Earth where the umbra falls, you would experience a total eclipse. If you were in the spot on Earth where the penumbra falls, you would experience a partial eclipse.

LOOKING AT A LUNAR ECLIPSE 342

What You'll Learn: A lunar eclipse occurs when the Earth blocks light to the moon.

Lunar eclipses don't happen very often, but when they do, they are exciting. Newspapers and television stations will inform you when one will occur in your area. We should not directly look at a solar eclipse, but it is safe to look at a lunar eclipse. When the next lunar eclipse occurs in your area, arrange to be in a place that offers a clear view, and watch as the eclipse takes place. You will clearly be able to see the shadow of the Earth slowly cross over the moon.

Weather and Seasons

Weather has a big impact on our lives. It influences the crops we grow,
how we dress, and even how we feel. When we talk about weather, we are talking
about changes that occur in the Earth's atmosphere from one day to the next.
The key parts of weather are temperature, the movement of air,
and the movement of water.

343 FLASH SUN

What You'll Learn: The Earth's tilt helps create the differences in the seasons.

What You'll Need: two similar flashlights

Many people think it is cold in the winter because the Earth is farther from the sun during the winter season. This is not true. In fact, in the Northern Hemisphere, the sun is slightly closer to the Earth during the winter. It is colder in the winter because the Earth tilts away from the sun and the sun's intensity on the Northern Hemisphere decreases.

To picture this, take two flashlights. Stand close to a wall. Shine one light straight at the wall. Notice the round circle of light it makes. Point the other flashlight slightly upward, and shine it against the wall. Notice the larger oval area of light it makes. Both flashlights put off the same light and heat, but the first one concentrates it in a smaller area, and the other one spreads the light and heat over a greater area.

344 THE HEAT IS ON

What You'll Learn: Land warms up faster than water.

What You'll Need: two containers; soil; water; two thermometers; tape; lamp; pen and paper; watch or clock

Fill a container halfway with soil. Fill another container one quarter of the way with water. Place a thermometer in each container just underneath the surface of the soil and water, and tape them into position on the sides of the containers. Check the temperature of the soil and of the water. Add more water to the container to make it half full and to make the water temperature the same as the soil temperature. If the water is cooler than the soil, add warm water; if the water is warmer than the soil, add cool water. Put a lamp over the containers so they both get the same amount of light and heat. Record the temperature every 2 minutes. Do this for about 20 minutes.

What Happened? The soil warmed at a faster rate than the water did. More energy is needed to raise the temperature of water than of land.

HOT AIR 345

What You'll Learn: Warm air rises.

What You'll Need: thermometer; pen and paper; stepladder

Use a thermometer to measure the air temperature near the floor in a room with poor air circulation, such as a garage. Write this down. Stand on a stepladder, and measure the temperature of the room at the highest point you can safely reach. Write this down. How are the temperatures different?

What Happened? The temperature near the ceiling was higher than the temperature near the floor because warm air is less dense than cold air, so it rises. This is an important principle in weather. When hot air rises, air from someplace else blows in. This movement creates wind and storms, which help to move moisture all across the Earth.

TURNTABLE WINDS

346

What You'll Learn: The Earth's rotation causes winds to shift direction, which affects weather patterns.

What You'll Need: paper; scissors; turntable, such as a lazy Susan, old record turntable, or microwave turntable; tape; ruler; marker; marble

Cut a circle from a sheet of paper about the same size as the turntable. Tape the paper circle to the surface of the turntable. Hold a ruler down on the paper, and draw a straight line as you have a friend slowly turn the turntable. Don't let the ruler turn. Look at the line. You'll see that the line is curved, even though you followed the edge of the ruler. Now rotate the turntable slowly, and roll a marble across it. Notice how the marble's straight line motion is curved by the rotation of the turntable.

What Happened? The turning of the table caused the marker line and marble to be deflected from their path across the paper. In a similar fashion, winds are deflected on Earth as the Earth rotates.

FAN OF THE WEATHER

347

What You'll Learn: Wind can have an effect on temperature.

What You'll Need: two thermometers; paper and pen; fan; glass of water; paper towel

Read and record the temperatures shown on two thermometers. Place one in the breeze of a fan and the other away from the fan. What do you think will happen to the temperature of the thermometer in the breeze? Many people might suspect that this thermometer will cool off and show a lower temperature. But as you will find, this does not occur. The breeze on the thermometer does not lower its temperature.

Allow a small glass of water to warm to room temperature. Wet a paper towel with this water. Place a small wad of the wet paper towel on the bulb of one thermometer. Do nothing to the second thermometer. Place both thermometers in the breeze of the fan. Record the temperatures every couple of minutes.

What Happened? The temperature of the thermometer with the wet towel on it dropped steadily. The breeze from the fan caused the water to evaporate, and as it evaporated, it used energy in the form of heat. This cooled the thermometer in the same way that your body cools itself when you perspire.

348 IT'S THE HUMIDITY

What You'll Learn: Humidity affects how hot we feel.

What You'll Need: paper and pen; weather reports

During the summer, make a chart with three columns; make the third column much wider than the first two. Label the first column "TEMPERATURE." Label the second column "HUMIDITY." Label the third column "HOW I FEEL." Each day for two weeks during the summer, find out the day's humidity and high temperature from the newspaper or television, and record these numbers in your chart. Also record how hot or uncomfortable the weather made you feel that day. Compare the information from the different days.

What Happened? If the temperature of two days is the same but the humidity is different, we would usually feel hotter on the day with the higher humidity. This happens because it is more difficult for the sweat of our bodies to evaporate on humid days. Normally sweat evaporates, cooling our bodies. But on humid days, the sweat evaporates slower, and we feel hotter.

CAN FROST 349

What You'll Learn: Frost forms because of a change in temperature.

What You'll Need: small metal can; water; salt; measuring spoon; crushed ice

Fill a small metal can one quarter of the way with water. Stir 4 tablespoons of salt into the water. Add enough crushed ice to fill the cup, and stir the solution. Observe what happens on the outside of the can.

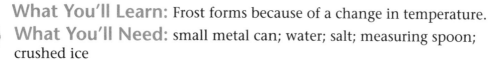

What Happened? The cold solution in the can lowered the temperature of the can. When the air outside the can came in contact with the cold can, the air's temperature also dropped. The amount of water vapor the air can hold depends on the air's temperature; it cannot hold as much water when it is cold. The water vapor condensed on the cold can, and the low temperature made the water freeze and form frost on the outside of the can.

NEWSPAPER WEATHER

350

What You'll Learn: The weather of places is influenced by where the places are located.

In the weather section of your newspaper, look at the big map of the United States. Choose some cities to keep track of their temperature highs. Choose one city far north, such as Albany, NY, and one far south, such as El Paso, TX. Choose one city by the ocean, such as San Diego, CA, and one city more inland, such as Phoenix, AZ. Choose one city high in the mountains, such as Denver, CO, and one city on low land, such as Kansas City, MO. Make a chart with the names of the cities down the side and the days of the week across the top. Use the chart to record the temperature of each city for one week.

What Happened? The temperature of each city changed during the week, but probably by only a few degrees. The northern city was probably colder than the southern city. The city near the ocean probably had less severe weather than the more inland city; if it was summer, it was not as hot, and if it was winter, it was not as cold. The city in the mountains was probably colder than the city on low land.

Rocks

Rocks are everywhere on Earth. We see them on the surface; we dig into the soil and find small rocks; we dig deeper and find bigger rocks. There are three basic types of rocks. *Igneous* rocks form when molten rock cools and hardens. *Sedimentary* rocks form when small rock particles are pressed together. *Metamorphic* rocks form when other rocks are put under great heat or pressure.

351 SAND MUSEUM

What You'll Learn: Sand is composed of tiny particles. These particles, or grains, are different sizes, colors, and shapes.

What You'll Need: sand; magnifying glass; dark construction paper; marker; glue

Lift some sand in your hand. Pour it out, and you'll see that it behaves almost like a liquid. Look at the sand using a magnifying glass. What does one sand grain look like? Compare it to others. Do they have different sizes, shapes, and colors?

Now make a sand museum. Find grains of as many different colors and sizes as you can. Draw squares on a piece of dark paper, and glue similar sand grains in the center of each square. Pretend they are rare jewels, and give them descriptive but fun names, such as the "Ruby Crystal" or the "Black Star."

WAY COOL: VOLCANIC ROCK 352

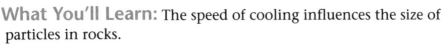

What You'll Learn: The speed of cooling influences the size of particles in rocks.

What You'll Need: volcanic rocks; magnifying glass

Examine different types of volcanic rocks closely. Use a magnifying glass to determine if each one is coarse or fine grained. The fine textures occur when the lava cools quickly, and the rough textures occur when the lava cools slowly.

353 FAST COOL, SLOW COOL

What You'll Learn: The speed of cooling influences the size of particles in rocks.

What You'll Need: metal container; bowl of ice; water; measuring cup and spoon; saucepan; stove; sugar; spoon; vanilla extract; salt

Caution: *This project requires adult supervision.*

Making candy is a sweet way to learn about rocks. The way you cool the candy influences the size of the candy particles. This is similar to how some rocks are formed.

Put a metal container into a large bowl filled with ice; you will use this cool container later. Bring ½ cup of water to a boil in a saucepan on the stove. Slowly add 2½ cups of sugar, mixing it gently with a spoon. Add 2 teaspoons of vanilla extract and ¼ teaspoon of salt. Keep stirring the candy mixture as you heat it. Heat the mixture to a slow boil until the sugar dissolves. Be careful that the solution does not foam up and out of the pan. When all of the sugar is dissolved, turn off the stove.

Now it's time to let the mixture cool. Take the container that you cooled with ice, and carefully pour half of the candy mixture into it. The cool container will make the candy solution cool quickly. Leave the remaining candy mixture in the pot, and put it in a safe spot to cool. It will cool more slowly than the other mixture. As the mixtures cool, they will form into crystals. Observe the size of the crystals in the two different containers.

What Happened? The candy that cooled quickly produced small crystals. It looked sandy or sugary. The candy that cooled slowly produced larger crystals. It produced lumpy candy. Rocks that are formed through heating and cooling behave the same way. Granite is an igneous rock with large grains, and basalt is an igneous rock with small grains. Do you think granite and basalt cooled at different rates? Which one cooled faster?

354 TOAST TO REGOLITH!

What You'll Learn: Regolith is a layer of loose rocks and soil that sits over solid rock. It is usually formed on Earth through erosion.

What You'll Need: toast; sandpaper

Make a piece of toast. Imagine that your toast is the hard, rocky surface of the Earth. Rub your hand on one side of the toast. Note the crumbs and fine particles that fall off. The friction from your hand caused the erosion of the toast. Rub the other side of the toast with sandpaper. The rough surface rubs off more particles. Friction from wind and water, from sand blown by the wind, and from rocks carried by glaciers can cause erosion in rocks and create pebbles, sand, and dirt. Some of this is washed away by water to lakes and oceans, and some of it remains on land. We call the layer of sediment that covers the ground *regolith*.

SEDIMENTAL JOURNEY 355

What You'll Learn: Materials in water settle at different rates.

What You'll Need: jar with lid; soil; sand; fine gravel; water

Put a handful of soil, sand, and fine gravel into a jar. Fill the jar with water, and screw the lid on tightly. Shake the jar so that all the materials are shaken up. Allow the contents of the jar to settle overnight. Check the jar, and observe the layers that were produced by the different materials.

What Happened? The soil, sand, and gravel all contained several different materials. The heavier materials sank to the bottom of the jar first. The lighter materials sank last. The different materials formed layers based on their weight. Thus, rocks were at the bottom, and clay particles were at the top. Some organic materials, such as leaves or twigs, might not have sunk at all. When water carries sediments to lakes and oceans, the sediments there form layers in the same way. Over time, pressure can force the particles together so they become sedimentary rocks.

TITE AND MITE

356

What You'll Learn: Stalactites and stalagmites are deposits of minerals that have been dissolved in water.

What You'll Need: two jars; water; Epsom salts; thick string; paper clips; jar lid

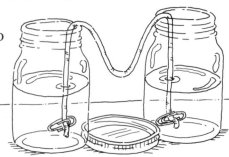

Fill two jars halfway with very warm water. Add as much Epsom salts as will dissolve in the water. Attach each end of a 3-foot piece of heavy string to a paper clip. Wet the entire string with the salt solution. Put one end of the string in one jar and the other end in the other jar, making sure the ends are covered by the liquid. Let the string hang between the two jars to form a loop. Place a jar lid under the loop. Observe every day for one week.

What Happened? As the string absorbed water from the jars, dissolved minerals from the Epsom salts were carried with the water through the string. They dripped off at the loop. As the water evaporated, the minerals were left behind and formed a stalactite (top) and a stalagmite (bottom). Stalactites and stalagmites form this way in caves when water that contains dissolved calcium drips from the cave ceiling.

ROCK AND ROLL

357

What You'll Learn: Weathering of rocks breaks them into smaller pieces.

What You'll Need: pebbles; water; jar with lid; coffee filters

Rinse all the dirt or debris from a handful of pebbles. Look at the pebbles, noting their size and shape. Place them in the jar, and add water until they are covered. Screw on the lid of the jar. Shake the jar, and swirl the rocks for a total of 20 minutes or more.

Observe the contents of the jar. Can you see small pieces of rock, sand, and clay that have broken off the pebbles? Place two coffee filters over the mouth of the jar. Pour off the water. Examine the pebbles and particles.

What Happened? The movement of the water broke the rock into smaller pieces. This kind of weathering happens in nature as water, wind, glaciers, and the Earth's shifting crust break down rocks into smaller pieces.

358 ACID TEST

What You'll Learn: Some rocks and minerals contain calcium carbonate.
What You'll Need: rocks; small cups; vinegar

Gather several small pieces of different kinds of rock. Place each piece into a different cup. Pour enough vinegar in each container to almost cover the rock. See if the rock starts fizzing. If it does, you'll know that the rock contains calcium carbonate; the acid in the vinegar reacts with the calcium carbonate to cause the fizzing. Rocks such as limestone, marble, calcite, and chalk react with the acid in this way. Acid rain can also break down rocks, just as vinegar can. Many ancient buildings and statues are made of marble, and acid rain is causing some of them to slowly dissolve.

SOFT AND HARD 359

What You'll Learn: Different minerals have different levels of hardness.
What You'll Need: talcum powder; gypsum (from drywall); penny; sandpaper

Hardness	Mineral
1	talc
2	gypsum
3	calcite
4	fluorite
5	apatite
6	feldspar
7	quartz
8	topaz
9	corundum
10	diamond

Different minerals have different levels of hardness. To measure hardness, geologists determine a mineral's resistance to scratching. Friedrich Mohs created a scale of hardness for classifying different minerals, which we call the Mohs' scale. You can see that talc is the softest mineral on the scale and diamond is the hardest.

Touch some talcum powder, and notice its softness. Then feel gypsum for its texture and hardness. Your fingernail can scratch minerals with a softness of about 2.5. A penny has a hardness of about 3. See if you can find minerals that can be scratched by a penny. Sandpaper is made with minerals such as corundum. These are very hard minerals. Gently touch your finger against some sandpaper to feel the hardness of these minerals.

Changes in the Earth

The surface of the Earth is always changing. Plates below the Earth's crust may push other plates up, forming mountain ranges and valleys. Volcanoes may erupt, forming mountains and islands. At the same time, forces also break down structures on Earth. Water seeps into rocks, freezes, and breaks the rocks. Wind, rain, and glaciers wear away rocky surfaces.

360 MY FAULT

What You'll Learn: Movement of the Earth's plates at fault lines causes changes in the Earth's surface.

What You'll Need: wooden plank; three colors of paint; paintbrush; saw

Caution: *This project requires adult supervision.*

Take a 2×4-inch piece of wood about 8 inches long. Paint three horizontal stripes of different colors on the 2-inch sides of the wood, and let the paint dry. These will represent layers of the Earth. Saw the wood in half at an angle. Paint the exposed inside sections of wood to match the other layers you painted, and let the paint dry. The wood represents Earth's plates, and the cut represents a fault line. You will use them to simulate earthquakes.

There are many ways that plates can move past each other on a fault line. Line up the cut ends of the wood. Starting with just a little pressure, push both blocks directly toward each other. Keep pushing until you get movement. One plate slides over the other plate. What geologic structures might this form? Line up the cut ends of the wood again. This time, slide your plates sideways. Some faults, such as the famous San Andreas Fault in California, cause this kind of movement.

361 PANGAEA PUZZLE

What You'll Learn: The continents of today may have been joined together in the past in one huge continent.

What You'll Need: world map; scissors

Find a map of the world that you can cut into pieces. Cut out all of the continents on the map. Think of them as pieces in a jigsaw puzzle. Try to fit the pieces together to form one big continent. Some scientists believe that the continents were once joined together in one huge landmass called Pangaea and that forces in the Earth caused them to drift apart over many millions of years. When you created the Pangaea Puzzle, the continents fit together pretty well, but not perfectly. If they had been joined together before, why wouldn't the pieces of your map fit together perfectly now?

BREAK OUT! 362

What You'll Learn: As ice forms, it can break up rocks.

Put an egg into the freezer for about five hours. Take it out, and carefully observe how it has changed.

What Happened? The egg broke open. When the materials inside the egg froze, they expanded and broke the hard outer shell of the egg. Similarly, when water gets into cracks in rocks and freezes, it expands and sometimes breaks the rocks. This is a type of weathering that can make changes in the features of the Earth's surface.

PLANTS DESTROY PARIS

363

What You'll Learn: As plants grow, they can break up rocks.

What You'll Need: dried kidney beans; paper cups; water; plaster of Paris

Put about five kidney beans into water, and allow them to soak for 1 hour. Mix up a small amount of plaster of Paris solution. Pour equal amounts of the plaster into two cups. Place the wet kidney beans in one cup. Add a few of drops of water to the surfaces of the plaster of Paris every day for several days. Observe what happens.

What Happened? On the first day, the plaster of Paris in the cup with the kidney beans was broken up. As the beans swelled from absorbing water, they caused cracks in the plaster. When you kept adding drops of water, some of the kidney beans grew through the cracks and caused the cracks to get bigger. The plaster of Paris in the other cup remained the same. Just as the kidney beans and plants cracked the plaster of Paris, plants in nature also grow roots into rocks and cause them to crack and break.

HIT THE BEACH

364

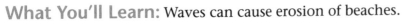

What You'll Learn: Waves can cause erosion of beaches.

What You'll Need: books; cake pan; sand; pebbles; water; sponge; soil

Put several books under one side of a rectangular cake pan so one side is raised a couple of inches. Put sand and pebbles on the raised end to form a beach. Put enough water in the pan so that it reaches the beach. Put a sponge in the other end of the pan. Push down on the sponge repeatedly to create small waves. Observe the effect the waves have on the sand and pebbles. Repeat the activity using soil. What does this activity tell you about beach erosion? Why are most waterfront areas made of sand and gravel instead of soil?

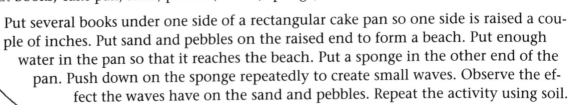

365 GRAZING GLACIERS

What You'll Learn: Glaciers erode land.

What You'll Need: gravel; paper cup; water; knife

Caution: *This project requires adult supervision.*

You are going to make a glacier. Put enough gravel in a paper cup to cover the bottom. Fill the cup three quarters of the way with water, and put it in the freezer. When the water is frozen, carefully cut away the bottom inch of paper from the cup. This exposes the ice and gravel but leaves a place for you to hold the ice. Find a patch of soil. Rub the ice and gravel part of your "glacier" over the soil. What effects did this have on the soil? During the last ice age, many places in the north were overrun with glaciers. The movement of these glaciers removed soil and rock and left deep gouges in the Earth.

INDEX